Mrs Beeton's
Favourite Party Dishes

Other Concorde Books

MRS BEETON'S FAVOURITE RECIPES
MRS BEETON'S FAVOURITE CAKES AND BREADS
MRS BEETON'S FAVOURITE SWEET DISHES
GARDENING FOR BEGINNERS
SIMPLE GREENHOUSE GARDENING
SIMPLE VEGETABLE GROWING
MAKING AND PLANNING A SMALL GARDEN
COLLECTING ANTIQUE SILVER
COLLECTING ANTIQUES

Peaches and pears in brandy-a dessert for a special occasion

Mrs Beeton's Favourite Party Dishes

Edited by
Maggie Black

Concorde Books

WARD LOCK LIMITED · LONDON

ACKNOWLEDGEMENTS

The Editor would like to thank all the people
and institutions who have supplied specialist
advice and pictures, and the manufacturers who
have advised on the use of modern food products.

The Fruit Producers' Council deserve special
thanks for their unfailing help in supplying
material on high-quality traditional products.

© Ward Lock Limited 1973

Paperback ISBN 0 7063 1201 5
Cased ISBN 0 7063 1204 X

First published in Great Britain 1973 by Ward
Lock Limited, 116 Baker Street, London, W1M
2BB

Designed by Andrew Vargo

Text in Baskerville (169/312)

Set and printed Offset Litho in England by
Cox & Wyman Ltd., London, Fakenham and
Reading

Contents

Weights and measures used in this book 6

Introduction 9

Ideas for special occasions 11

Dishes for dinner parties 23

The wedding 45

Christmas and other traditional festivities 48

Festivity menus 57

Special festival cakes 58

Children's parties 63

Teen-agers' parties 71

Informal parties 81

Pancake parties 81

Alfresco parties 86

Barbecues 94

Winter evening parties 97

Supper parties 100

Supper 'before a show' 100

Late night parties 103

Coffee and tea parties 108

Basic recipes 117

Index 125

Weights and Measures Used in this Book

Liquid measures

60 drops	1 teaspoon
3 teaspoons	1 tablespoon
4 tablespoons	$\frac{1}{2}$ gill
1 gill	$\frac{1}{4}$ pint
4 gills	1 pint
2 pints	1 quart
4 quarts	1 gallon

Homely solid measures

Spoons are British Standard teaspoons and tablespoons, which hold the amounts of liquid given above. They are measured with the contents levelled off, i.e. all the spoonfuls are level spoonfuls.

The cup is a British Standard measuring cup which holds 10 fluid oz or an Imperial $\frac{1}{2}$ pint.

Flour, sifted	3 tablespoons	1 oz
Castor or granulated sugar	2 tablespoons	$1\frac{1}{4}$ oz
Icing sugar, sifted	3 tablespoons	1 oz
Butter or margarine	2 tablespoons	$1\frac{1}{4}$ oz
Cornflour	2 tablespoons	1 oz
Granulated or powdered gelatine	4 teaspoons	$\frac{1}{2}$ oz
Golden syrup or treacle	1 tablespoon	1 oz
Flour, sifted	1 cup	5 oz
Castor or granulated sugar	1 cup	9 oz
Icing sugar, sifted	1 cup	5 oz
Butter or margarine	1 cup	9 oz
Cornflour	1 cup	8 oz
Golden syrup or treacle	1 cup	1 lb

Metric measures

Precise metric equivalents are not very useful. The weights are almost impossible to measure accurately, and are not used in ordinary cooking. Schools use a 25-gram unit for 1 oz and for re-tested recipes. This means that they can use existing equipment. For instance, a 6-inch sandwich tin can be used for a 15-cm one, and a 7-inch tin for an 18-cm one. Yorkshire pudding using 100 grams plain flour fits into a 2 × 14 cm (8 in × $5\frac{1}{2}$ in) baking tin. Mrs Beeton's recipes are all being re-tested so that they can be converted to metric measures when these come into general use.

Oven temperatures

	Electric	Celsius	Gas
Very cool	225 °F	110 °C	$\frac{1}{4}$
Very cool	250 °F	130 °C	$\frac{1}{2}$
Very cool	275 °F	140 °C	1
Cool	300 °F	150 °C	2
Warm	325 °F	170 °C	3
Moderate	350 °F	180 °C	4
Fairly hot	375 °F	190 °C	5
Fairly hot	400 °F	200 °C	6
Hot	425 °F	220 °C	7
Very hot	450 °F	230 °C	8
Very hot	475 °F	240 °C	9

Deep fat frying table

Food	Bread Browns In	Fat Temp	Oil Temp
Uncooked mixtures, e.g. fritters	1 minute	370–375 °F	375–385 °F
Cooked mixtures, e.g. fish cakes	40 seconds	380–385 °F	385 °F
Fish	1 minute	375 °F	375 °F
Potato straws' chips, etc	20 seconds	390 °F	395 °F

Introduction

MOST PEOPLE HAVE to give parties from time to time.

Within a family, for instance, the traditional festivals such as Christmas and Easter usually call for some kind of family gathering, which often includes friends as well. So do children's birthdays. A wedding is nearly always celebrated with a party of some kind.

Other personal and family occasions which are often marked by a party include a 21st birthday, an engagement, and a silver wedding. Many people, too, like to commemorate an occasion such as moving into a new home by giving a party.

We give many other kinds of parties as well, which are not linked to special occasions. A good many people need to give cocktail, lunch or dinner parties at home for business reasons. Others give them just to bring friends together, or to return the hospitality of others. It may also be convenient to give guests a meal at home before taking them to the theatre, or afterwards. Young people especially sometimes like to have their friends round on a Sunday morning for brunch or lunch, to swim or play tennis. More formally, older people may well invite others to talk business over lunch; or they may meet for a club lunch, or just a social one. A willing hostess may also find herself giving various other kinds of parties for a club or society, from a fund-raising 'coffee morning' to evening refreshments after a lecture.

Then, besides all these 'parties for a reason', there are many parties which people give just because they like doing it: pancake parties, wine and cheese parties, beer and sausage parties, TV parties and a great many others.

This book is designed to help any party-giver with ideas and recipes for many and various occasions, whether it means feeding more people than usual with easy dishes to do 'for a crowd' or providing guests with more elaborate or formal dishes than in an everyday meal. Since every hostess secretly hopes to impress her guests, these dishes are designed to make a memorable meal.

But the overall idea behind all the recipes and menus is to make the hostess's task easy. A gay, confident hostess creates the right atmosphere for a good party. A tired or harassed one often fails. So this book aims to make party-giving pleasant and simple, so that the hostess enjoys her own party, and provides an enjoyable occasion.

Ideas for Special Occasions

AVOCADO PEARS AND PRAWNS

2 large Avocado pears	Crisp lettuce leaves
2 tablesp olive oil	Lemon
2 tablesp vinegar	Pinch of sugar (optional)
Good pinch of salt	
Good pinch of pepper	¼ crushed clove of garlic (optional)
A little mixed mustard	
2 teacups (about ½ pt) shelled prawns	

Halve the pears. Blend the oil, vinegar and seasonings together. Toss the prawns in this, and then spoon into the pear halves. Put on to crisp lettuce leaves and garnish with wedges of lemon.

A pinch of sugar can be added to the dressing if wished, also a little garlic.

4 helpings

ASPARAGUS—'AU NATUREL'

1 bundle of asparagus	2 oz butter
Salt	Lemon juice

Trim the hard white ends of the asparagus to suitable lengths for serving. Scrape the stalks with a sharp knife, working down-wards from the head. Wash them well in cold water. Tie them into small bundles with the heads in one direction. Re-trim the stalks evenly. Keep them in cold water until ready to cook. Cook very gently, with the heads off the source of heat, in just enough salted boiling water to cover. When tender (in about 15–20 min), drain and serve on a folded table napkin. Serve with melted butter, seasoned and lightly fla-voured with lemon.

Note: To ensure that the tender point of the asparagus is not overcooked by the time that the stem is ready, thin asparagus should be cooked 'standing'. This can be achieved in an 'asparagus boiler', a narrow, very deep pan. A bottling jar half-filled with boiling water, stood in a deep sauce-pan of boiling water, serves as a very good substitute. The asparagus is placed stems down in the jar, and the points cook more slowly in steam only. Allow 30 min for this method of cooking.

Allow 6 or 8 medium-sized heads per person

GLOBE ARTICHOKES WITH HOLLANDAISE SAUCE

6 globe artichokes	½ pt Hollandaise sauce
Salt	
1 tablesp lemon juice	*or* 2 oz melted butter

Asparagus 'au naturel'

Soak the artichokes in cold, salt water for at least 1 hr, to ensure the removal of all dust and insects. Wash them well. Cut off the tails and trim the bottoms with a sharp knife. Cut off the outer leaves and trim the tops of the remaining ones with scissors. Put them into a pan with just sufficient boiling water to cover them, adding salt and the lemon juice. Cook until tender, 15–45 min, according to size and freshness (when cooked leaves pull out easily). Test frequently after 15 min as they are apt to break and become discoloured if over-cooked. Remove from water and drain them well by turning them upside down. Serve with Hollandaise sauce or melted butter.

HOLLANDAISE SAUCE

2 tablesp wine vinegar	Salt and pepper
2 egg yolks	Lemon juice
2–4 oz butter	

Boil the vinegar till it is reduced by half; allow to cool. Mix the cool vinegar with the egg yolks in a basin and place this over hot water. Whisk the egg yolks till they begin to thicken, then whisk in the butter gra-

dually until all is absorbed. Season, add lemon juice to taste and serve immediately.

STUFFED ARTICHOKE BOTTOMS

Artichoke bottoms	1 tablesp of
Butter *or*	stuffing for each
margarine	(approx)

Where economy does not matter, globe artichokes may be cooked as in the preceding recipe and only the bottoms or 'fonds' used. After cooking, the leaves are carefully pulled out of the artichokes so that the bottoms are retained, unbroken.

Stuffings

1 Cooked rice well seasoned and flavoured with cheese, preferably Parmesan *or*
2 Fried, finely chopped shallot, young cooked peas, mint, seasoning *or*
3 Cooked sausage meat, chopped chives, French mustard *or*
4 Finely chopped fried onion, mushroom, and a little tomato purée.
Toss the cooked artichoke bottoms in hot butter or margarine. Pile the hot, well-flavoured stuffing on each bottom. Serve immediately. Allow 1 artichoke bottom for each person.

Cooking time 5–7 min to fry the bottoms

CONSOMMÉ MADRILÈNE

1 qt brown stock	1 bay leaf
1 lb tomatoes	$\frac{1}{4}$–$\frac{1}{2}$ lb lean beef
1 green pepper	1 carrot
1 clove of garlic	1 egg white
Parsley stalks	1 onion
Thyme	1 stick of celery

Cut up the tomatoes and green pepper. Tie the herbs together in a small piece of muslin. Shred and soak the beef in $\frac{1}{4}$ pt water. Whip the egg white slightly. Put all ingredients into a pan and simmer very gently for 1 hr. Strain as usual. To garnish cut tiny dice from the firm flesh of skinned tomato. Serve the consommé hot or iced; if iced, it should be almost liquid and may therefore need whisking a little.

6 helpings

DEVILLED LOBSTER

boiled lobster	2 tablesp white
butter	sauce *or* cream
3 tablesp white	Cayenne pepper
breadcrumbs	A few browned
	breadcrumbs

Cut the lobster in two lengthwise, remove
the meat carefully, as the ½ shell must be
kept whole, and chop the meat finely.
Melt 1½ oz butter and pour it on the lobster.
Add the white breadcrumbs, and the sauce,
season rather highly with cayenne and mix
well. Press the mixture lightly into the
shells, cover with browned breadcrumbs,
put 3 or 4 pieces of butter on top and bake
or about 20 min in a moderate oven
180 °C, 350 °F, Gas 4). Serve hot or cold.

helpings

Globe artichokes

LOBSTER THERMIDOR

small boiled	Pinch of cayenne
lobsters	pepper
shallot	A little grated
wine glass white	cheese
wine	Parsley to
½ oz butter	garnish
¼ pt Béchamel	
sauce	
level teasp	
mixed mustard	

Cut the lobsters in half lengthwise and remove the stomach and the intestinal cord.
Remove the meat from the shell and cut
into slices, keeping the knife on the slant.
Chop the shallot very finely. Put the white
wine in a small saucepan and cook the
shallot until it is tender and the wine
reduced to half. Meanwhile, melt the butter and heat the meat very carefully in
this. Add the shallot and wine mixture to
the lobster meat with the sauce, mustard
and pepper, mix and return to the shells.
Sprinkle with grated cheese and brown
under a hot grill. Serve garnished with
parsley and accompanied by a simple
salad or plain lettuce.

helpings

CHATEAUBRIAND STEAK

A double fillet	Olive oil *or*
steak not less	melted butter
than 1¼ in thick	Salt and pepper

Wipe the steak. Remove any sinew or
skin. Cover the meat with a cloth and beat
lightly to flatten. Brush over with oil or
melted butter and season. Place under a
red-hot grill and cook both sides quickly;
the steak should be well browned but
slightly underdone. Serve immediately on
a hot dish with potato straws. Serve also
Maître d'Hôtel butter and gravy, or demi-
glace, tomato or Béchamel sauce.

TOURNEDOS OF BEEF, ROSSINI

1½ lb fillet of beef,	1 tablesp brown
cut as tournedos	sauce
¼ lb chickens'	Salt and pepper
livers	1 tablesp olive
2 oz butter *or* fat	oil
1 shallot	Meat glaze
1½ oz foie gras or	Croûtes of fried
pâté	bread
	½–¾ pt demi-glace
	sauce

Wipe the beef and cut into rounds 2½ in diameter and ½ in thick; that is, cut as tournedos. Wash, dry and slice the livers. Melt 1 oz of the fat in a sauté pan and fry the finely-chopped shallot slightly. Add the liver and sauté for a few minutes. Drain off the fat and pound the livers with the foie gras or pâté, brown sauce and seasoning until smooth, then pass through a wire sieve. Heat the remainder of the fat with the olive oil and fry the tournedos quickly until browned on both sides. Drain and cover one side of each with the liver farce. Brush with meat glaze, place on the fried croûtes and put in the oven to become thoroughly hot. Arrange the fillets on a hot dish and serve the demi-glace sauce separately.

6 helpings

CROWN ROAST OF LAMB WITH SAFFRON RICE

A 2-section crown	Salt
roast of lamb	Pepper
Oil for brushing	

STUFFING

1 oz butter	2 oz frozen peas
1 stick celery,	1 oz chopped,
chopped	blanched
1 onion, chopped	almonds
5 oz long-grain	2 dessert apples,
white rice	cored and diced
½ gill dry white	1 oz butter
wine	
1 pt chicken stock,	
heated, with a	
scant ¼ teasp	
powdered saffron	

Ask the butcher to prepare the crown roast. Place the joint in a roasting tin. Brush with oil and season well with salt and pepper. Wrap a small piece of foil around the top of each rib to prevent it from scorching during cooking. Cook at 190°C, 375°F, Gas 5, for 1¼–1½ hr. Approx 30 min before the joint is due to finish cooking, prepare the saffron rice stuffing by melting the butter in a saucepan and cooking the celery and onion until soft but not browned. Stir in the raw rice and cook for 1–2 min. Pour on the wine and cook gently until the rice has absorbed it. Add ½ pt of the saffron-flavoured chicken stock and cook, uncovered, stirring occasionally, until almost all the liquid is absorbed. Pour the remaining stock over the rice and cook until it has been completely absorbed and the rice is just tender. Remove from the heat and add the peas, chopped nuts, diced apple and butter and cover the saucepan with fitting lid.

Drain the joint and place on a warmed serving-dish. Remove the foil from the rib bones. Fill the roast with the hot saffron rice. Top each rib with a cutlet frill and serve. (Any extra rice can be served separately.)

6–8 helpings

SCALLOPS EN BROCHETTE

4 large scallops	8 small rashers
6 oz rice	streaky bacon
	4 thick slices
	pineapple

Scallops are usually opened by the fishmonger and displayed in their flat shells. If the scallops are to be served in their shells ask the fishmonger for the *deep* shells. If however it is necessary to open scallops they should be put over a gentle heat to allow the shells to open. When they have opened remove from the shells, trim away the beard and remove the black parts. Wash the scallops well, drain and dry. Wash and dry the shells; keep the deep shells for serving dishes. Scallops are in season from November to March. They can be served baked, fried, poached or grilled as follows. Cook the rice in fast-boiling salted water until just tender. Wash the scallops and cut in half, then roll each half in a rasher of bacon. Impale on a thin skewer with a half slice of pineapple between each. Grill under a moderate heat, turning once, for 8–10 min. Drain the rice when cooked, rinse under running cold water, then spread out on a sieve and reheat. Pile up on a dish and lay the 4 skewers on the rice. Serve hot.

4 helpings

GREY MULLET OR TROUT EN PAPILLOTES

| 4 grey mullet *or* trout | 1 tablesp lemon juice |
| salt and pepper | |

Prepare the fish, sprinkle the insides with salt and pepper and wrap carefully in well-oiled greaseproof paper or aluminium foil, twisting the ends securely. Place on a baking-sheet and bake for about 15–20 min in a fairly hot oven (190 °C, 375 °F, Gas 5). When cooked, loosen the paper carefully and place the fish on a hot dish. Add the lemon juice to the liquid which has collected in the paper, pour this over the fish and serve. Garnish with slices of lemon and sprigs of parsley.

If liked, the mullet or trout may be stuffed with a mixture of 1 oz fresh breadcrumbs, ½ level tablesp grated onion, 1 level dessertsp chopped parsley, salt and pepper to taste, moistened with a little milk. Allow a little longer cooking time.

4 helpings

TROUT 'AU BLEU'

| One 6–8 oz trout | Salt |
| Vinegar | Parsley |

The essential factor of this famous dish is that the trout should be alive until just before cooking. In restaurants they are often kept in a tank from which the customer selects his fish. The fish should be stunned, cleaned (gutted) and immediately plunged into a pan of boiling salted water to which a little vinegar has been added. (The fish are not scaled or washed as this would spoil the blue colour.) Draw the pan aside, or reduce the heat, and poach the fish for about 10–12 min. Drain, and serve garnished with parsley and accompanied by melted butter, Hollandaise sauce and small boiled potatoes.

LOBSTER—HOW TO CHOOSE

Lobsters can be obtained all the year round, but are scarce from December to March. They are cheapest during the summer months. Lobsters are usually bought already boiled, but live lobsters can be obtained to order if a few days' notice is given to the fishmonger. Choose one of medium size and heavy in weight. If fresh, the tail of a cooked lobster will be stiff; if gently raised, it will return with a spring. The narrowness of the back part of the tail and the stiffness of the two uppermost fins (swimmerettes) in the tail distinguish the cock lobster from the hen.

BOILING A LOBSTER

There are two methods of boiling lobsters, each method having points in its favour.

Method 1
Wash the lobster well before boiling, tie the claws securely. Have ready a saucepan of boiling water, salted in the proportion of ¼ lb salt to 1 gallon water. Throw the lobster head first into the water (this instantly destroys life), keep it boiling for 20–45 min, according to size, and skim well. Allow 20 min–½ hr for small lobsters and ½–¾ hr for large lobsters. If boiled too long the meat becomes thready, and if not done enough, the coral is not red. If serving in the shell, rub the shells over with a little salad oil to brighten the colour.

Method 2
Put the lobsters into warm water, bring the water gradually to the boil and boil as above. This is believed by many to be a more humane method of killing, as the lobster is lulled to sleep and does not realize it is being killed.

PREPARING A LOBSTER FOR EATING

Wipe the lobster well with a clean damp cloth and twist off claws and legs. Place lobster on a board parallel to the edge with back uppermost and head to the left. Cut along the centre of back, from junction of head with body to tail, using a sharp, stainless knife. Reverse so that tail is to left and cut along head; the stomach, which lies just behind the mouth, is not cut until last. Remove intestinal cord, remove stomach and coral (if any) and keep for garnish. The meat may be left in the shell or removed and used as required. To remove the meat, knock tips of the claws

Preparing trout en papillotes

Châteaubriand steak

with the back of a knife and drain away any water. Tap sharply round the broadest part of each claw and the shell should fall apart. Cut the cartilage between pincers, open the pincers and the meat can be removed in one piece. Remove the meat from the smaller joints of claws.

SALMI OF PHEASANT

1 pheasant	½ pt brown sauce
2 oz butter	1 glass Madeira
¼ teasp grated	(optional)
lemon rind	6–8 slices goose
2 shallots	liver *or* pâté
¼ teasp thyme	6–8 mushrooms
1 bay leaf	Salt and pepper

GARNISH
Croûtes of fried bread (triangular) *or* **fleurons of puff pastry**

Pluck, draw and truss bird for roasting. Baste it well with hot butter; roast in a hot oven (220–230 °C, 425–450 °F, Gas 7–8) for 30 min, basting frequently. Pour the butter used for basting into a saucepan, add grated lemon rind, chopped shallots, thyme and bay leaf. Joint the bird, lay aside breast, wings, and legs, and cut remainder into neat pieces; add these to the saucepan and fry. If any fat remains, pour it from the saucepan, put in the brown sauce, wine (if used), and season. Simmer for 10 min. Add remainder of pheasant, heat thoroughly. Meanwhile, reheat the butter, fry in it the slices of goose liver if used, and the mushrooms. Correct seasoning of sauce

Crown roast of lamb with saffron rice

Serve pheasant with pâté or liver; strain the sauce over, garnish with the croûtes or fleurons and the mushrooms.

4–5 helpings Cooking time—about 1¼ hr in all

GROUSE PIE

2 grouse	Salt and pepper
¾ lb rump steak	½ pt good stock
2–3 slices of bacon	Puff pastry,
2 hard-boiled eggs	frozen *or* using
	8 oz flour, etc

Joint the birds, and discard vent-end parts of the backs, as these will impart a bitter flavour to the pie. Slice the steak thinly, slice eggs and cut the bacon into strips. Line the bottom of a pie dish with pieces of seasoned meat, cover with a layer of grouse, add some bacon, egg and seasoning. Repeat until dish is full. Add sufficient stock to ¾ fill the pie dish, cover with puff pastry as above and bake for 1½–1¾ hr. For the first 15 min of this time, have the oven hot (220–230°C, 425–450°F, Gas 7–8), then lower the heat to moderate (180–190°C, 350–375°F, Gas 4–5) and cover the pastry with greaseproof paper so that

17

the filling may cook a further 1¼–1½ hr. Glaze the pie ½ hr before cooking is complete. Simmer the necks and trimmings of the birds in the remaining stock, strain, season and pour into the pie before serving. Finely chopped mushrooms, parsley and shallots may be added to the pie, if liked.

6–8 helpings   *Cooking time—1¾ hr*

ARTICHOKE BOTTOMS WITH BÉCHAMEL SAUCE

6 artichoke bottoms	½ pt Béchamel sauce
2 oz butter *or* margarine	

Trim the cooked artichoke bottoms and, if large, cut in halves. Toss in hot butter or margarine. Season and serve with hot Béchamel sauce.

4–6 helpings   Cooking time—7 min to fry the bottoms

STEAMED CUCUMBER WITH WHITE SAUCE

2 large cucumbers	¾ pt white sauce
1 oz butter *or* margarine	1 egg
1 teasp finely chopped shallot	1 teasp finely chopped parsley
	Salt and pepper

Peel the cucumber and steam it until tender (about 20 min). Drain well and cut into 1 in slices. Melt the butter in a saucepan, put in the shallot and cook it without browning. Add the sliced cucumber, toss over heat for a few minutes, then stir in the white sauce. Just before boiling point is reached, add the well-beaten egg and parsley, stir and cook gently until the egg thickens. Season and serve hot.

6 helpings

GREEN PEAS, FRENCH STYLE

2 lb green peas (1½ pt shelled peas)	2 oz butter *or* margarine
4 very small onions *or* spring onions	2 teasp sugar
	Salt and pepper
1 lettuce	Egg yolk (optional)

Shell the peas. Peel the onions. Remove the outer leaves of the lettuce, wash the heart, leaving it whole. Put the peas into a thick saucepan, add the lettuce heart, onions and the butter cut into small pieces. Stir in the sugar and a little salt. Cover with the lid and cook over a very low heat, about 1 hr, shaking the pan occasionally. Re-season and serve. The liquid in the pan may be thickened with an egg yolk before serving.

6 helpings

POACHED SPINACH

3 lb spinach	2 tablesp cream (optional)
1 oz butter *or* margarine	Salt and pepper

Pick over the spinach carefully and wash it in at least 3 waters. Break off the stalks and at the same time pull off the central ribs if coarse. (Young, summer spinach need not be stripped of the central ribs.) Put the wet leaves into a saucepan, without additional water. Cook slowly until tender, about 15 min, stirring the spinach in the pan occasionally. The pan should have a tightly fitting lid. Drain well, pressing out the water. Re-heat in the butter. Add the cream, if used, and mix it well with the spinach. Season and serve hot.
For spinach purée, drain the cooked spinach well and sieve it or purée in an electric blender before adding the cream.

5–6 helpings

ANNA POTATOES

2 lb even-sized waxy potatoes	Salt and pepper Melted clarified butter *or* margarine

Grease a thick cake-tin and line the bottom with greased paper. Peel and trim the potatoes so that they will give equal sized slices. Slice them very finely and arrange a layer of slightly overlapping slices. Sprinkle with clarified fat and seasoning. Make a second layer of potato and repeat. Continue until the tin is full, pressing each layer well into the tin. Cover with greased paper and a lid and bake in a fairly hot oven (190 °C, 375 °F, Gas 5) for about 1 hr. Look at the potatoes from time to time and add more clarified butter if they become dry. Turn out on to a hot dish and serve at once.

6 helpings   *Cooking time—about 1 hr*

SAUTÉED POTATOES

6 medium-sized potatoes (waxy ones)	1–2 oz butter *or* margarine Seasoning

Cook the potatoes, preferably in their skins, until only just soft. Let them dry thoroughly then peel and slice them $\frac{1}{4}$ in thick. Heat the fat in a frying-pan and put in the potatoes. Season them with salt and pepper. Toss in the fat until they are light brown and have absorbed all the fat. Serve at once.

4–6 helpings

POTATO CHIPS and POTATO STRAWS

6 medium-sized potatoes	Deep fat Salt

Scrub and rinse the potatoes. Peel them thinly. For chips—cut into sticks about 2 in long and $\frac{1}{4}$ in wide and thick. For straws—cut into strips the size of a wooden match. Drop them into cold water as they are cut. Rinse and drain and dry in a clean cloth. Put them into the frying-basket and lower them gently into hot deep fat at 180 °C, 360 °F. (Keep the heat fairly high as the potatoes will have cooled the fat.) When the potatoes are soft but *not* brown—about 3 min for chips and 1 min for straws—lift out the basket and heat the fat to 190 °C, 375 °F. Put back the basket and leave in the fat until the potatoes are crisp and golden brown—about 3 min for chips and 2 min for straws.
Drain on absorbent paper, sprinkle with salt and serve immediately.
Note: If potato chips or straws are to be served with fried fish or any other fried dish, the second frying of the potatoes to brown and crisp them should be done after the fish, etc., is fried. In this way the potatoes will be sent to table in their best condition.

6 helpings   *Cooking time—for chips, about 6 min, for straws, about 3 min*

MILANAISE SOUFFLÉ

2 lemons
3–4 eggs,
according to size
5 oz caster sugar
$\frac{1}{2}$ oz gelatine
$\frac{1}{4}$ pt water
$\frac{1}{2}$ pt double cream

DECORATION
Chopped pistachio nuts

Wash lemons dry, and grate rind finely. Whisk the egg yolks, sugar, rind and lemon juice over hot water until thick and creamy, then remove bowl from the hot water and continue whisking until cool. Soften the gelatine in the $\frac{1}{4}$ pt water, and heat to dissolve. Half-whip the cream. Whisk the egg whites very stiffly. Add the gelatine, still hot, in a thin stream, to the egg mixture, and stir in as you do it. Fold in the cream and the stiffly-whipped whites. Fold the mixture very lightly until setting is imminent, when the mixture pulls against the spoon. Pour into the soufflé dish and leave to set. Remove the paper band by coaxing it away from the mixture with a knife dipped in hot water. Decorate the sides with chopped, blanched pistachio nuts, and the top with whipped cream, if liked.
This is a good 'basic' soufflé recipe. It can be flavoured and decorated with almost any flavouring and garnish, such as coffee, chocolate, fruit or a liqueur, with appropriate small sweets or nuts as decoration.

6 helpings   *Setting time—2 hr*

Note: Tie a double band of greaseproof paper round a 1 pt china soufflé dish, so that 3 in of the paper extends above the rim. This makes a mould in which the soufflé mixture will set 1–1$\frac{1}{2}$ in above the rim, and on removal of the paper, will appear to have 'risen' above the dish.

Salmi of pheasant with croûtes

Sautéed potatoes

HAWAIIAN DREAMS

1 large can crushed pineapple	2 oz chopped browned almonds
½ oz gelatine	¼ pt sweetened whipped cream
2 teasp lemon juice	6–8 maraschino cherries
1 pt vanilla or chocolate ice cream	

Measure the crushed pineapple and make it up to 1 pt with water. Dissolve the gelatine in a little of the liquid but do not allow to boil. Add it to the crushed pineapple with the lemon juice. Pour into individual glasses to set. Just before serving, place a scoop of ice cream on top of the set mixture. Sprinkle with nuts. Decorate with a rose of cream and place a cherry on top.

6 individual glasses

Hawaiian dreams

Milanaise soufflé

and of the consistency of marshmallow in the centre. Cool and remove very carefully on to a flat cake-tray or board. Fill and serve cut in wedges.

PAVLOVA CAKE

3 egg whites	½ teasp cornflour
6 oz castor sugar	½ teasp vinegar
½ teasp vanilla essence	Filling as below

Beat the egg whites until stiff. Continue beating, gradually adding the sugar. Beat until sugar is dissolved and at this stage the mixture should be very stiff and standing well in peaks. Fold in vanilla, cornflour and vinegar. Spread mixture in a 6–8 in circle on greaseproof paper on a baking-sheet, making the sides higher than the centre to form a shell to hold filling. Place in a cool oven at 150 °C, 300 °F, Gas 2, for 1–1½ hr. The pavlova should be crisp and very lightly tinted on the surface yet remain soft

FILLING

Pile ½ pt whipped and flavoured cream into the pavlova shell and on top of this arrange a selection of fruit: pineapple; strawberries or other berry fruits; cherries; apricots; mandarins; passion fruit; grapes; fresh or canned peaches, etc., according to taste and season. Finally decorate with angelica, maraschino cherries or almonds as desired.

There are many other pavlova filling mixtures. Try blackcurrants with a little cassis liqueur, or pear slices and raspberries with lemon juice.

Note: You can also decorate the shell in various ways. Use a fancy forcing pipe to make small rosettes on the sides, for instance.

CREPES SUZETTE

½ pt pancake batter	Icing sugar
	Brandy *or* rum
FILLING	
2 oz butter	2 teasp orange juice
3 oz castor sugar	1 teasp lemon juice
Grated rind of ½ orange	1 tablesp Kirsch *or* Curaçao

Make the batter, and leave it to stand. Cream together the butter and sugar for the filling until very soft. Then work in the orange juice, rind, lemon juice and liqueur. Make a very thin pancake, spread with some filling, roll up and dredge with icing sugar. Put into a warm place while making the rest of the pancakes, and filling them. Just before serving, pour the warmed brandy or rum over the pancakes and light it. Serve immediately.

If you prefer, warm the filling with the brandy until liquid, and pour it over the unfilled pancakes folded over twice. Light and serve.

PEACHES PRESERVED IN BRANDY

Peaches	Water
Sugar	Brandy

Dip peaches in hot water, one at a time, and rub off the 'fur' with clean towel. Weigh. For each lb fruit allow ¾ lb sugar and 8 oz (in a measuring jug) water. Boil the sugar and water together for 10 min without stirring. Add the peaches to the syrup and cook (only a few at a time to prevent bruising) for about 5 min until tender. Remove the peaches from the syrup with a strainer and pack firmly into hot sterilised jars. Continue cooking the syrup, after removing peaches, until thick. Cool and measure. Add equal quantity of brandy. Bring to boiling point and fill jars of peaches to overflowing. Seal.

The following sweets can be served with coffee:

PEPPERMINT CREAMS

1 lb icing sugar	1–2 drops oil of peppermint *or* 2 teasp peppermint essence
Whites of 2 large eggs	

Sieve the icing sugar and add the stiffly beaten egg whites and the peppermint flavouring. A very little green colour may be added if liked. Mix all well together to a firm dough-like ball and roll out, well sifted with icing sugar, to about ⅛–¼ in thick. Cut out with a small round sweet cutter and leave on a wire tray to dry out for 12 hr. Pack into an air-tight container. The creams may be coated with melted chocolate if desired. For this, dissolve some broken chocolate in a bowl over hot water and dip the creams into the chocolate, holding them on a fine skewer or a sweet-dipping fork.

Decorate with crystallised rose or violet petals, sugar mimosa or flaked almonds. Allow to set on clean greaseproof paper before placing in sweet cases.

DATES

Dates can be served plain or stuffed. To stuff: slit the date and remove the stone. Fill the cavity with a whole blanched almond or roll of marzipan. Roll in castor sugar.

MARZIPAN

1 lb loaf sugar	2 egg whites
1½ gills water	3 oz sifted icing sugar
12 oz ground almonds	Flavouring

Boil the loaf sugar and water to 240 °F, then draw the sugar boiler or pan aside, and when the syrup has cooled slightly add the almonds and egg whites. Stir over a low heat for a few minutes, then turn on to a slab, stir in the icing sugar, and work with a palette knife until cool enough to handle. Knead with the hands until perfectly smooth, add flavouring and colouring. Mould into small balls and press half a walnut into each or shape as miniature fruit, etc.

Dishes for Dinner Parties

GRAPEFRUIT BASKETS

½ grapefruit per person	4–6 fresh orange segments per person
1 wedge fresh melon per person	3 maraschino cherries per person
4–6 pineapple chunks per person (fresh or canned)	
Sugar to taste	
1 sprig fresh mint per person	

Halve each grapefruit. Remove the sections and skin them. Discard core and pips. Mix the skinned sections with diced melon, pineapple and skinned section of fresh orange. Add halves maraschino cherries. Flavour with sugar to taste, but do not make too sweet. Replace the fruit in the grapefruit skins. Chill. When required, top each grapefruit half with a sprig of mint. Serve in individual bowls or champagne glasses.

PRAWN COCKTAIL

Heart of a small lettuce	1 teasp chilli vinegar—if available
½ pt picked prawns	1 teasp tarragon vinegar
½ gill mayonnaise	

Dressed crab

1 tablesp tomato purée (*see* **below**) *or* **tomato ketchup**	**Good pinch of salt**
	Good pinch of cayenne pepper
	Lemon

Wash and dry the lettuce very well—pick out the tiny leaves and break into very small pieces. Arrange in cocktail glasses. Put the prawns on top. Mix the mayonnaise with the tomato ketchup or purée—to obtain this rub one large tomato through a fine sieve. Add the vinegars and seasoning. Put over the prawns and garnish with a piece of lemon and a dusting of cayenne pepper.
Serve very cold.

4 helpings

POTTED SHRIMPS

1 pt shrimps— measure when shelled	**Pinch of salt**
	Grating of nutmeg
2–3 oz butter	**Lettuce**
Good pinch of cayenne pepper	**Lemon**

Heat the butter and turn the shrimps in this until they are well coated, but do not cook them. Add the seasonings and nutmeg. Pour into small moulds or dishes and leave until the butter is set. Turn out on to a bed of crisp lettuce and garnish with lemon. Serve with cayenne pepper and crisp toast.

DRESSED CRAB

One 2½–3 lb crab	**A little lemon juice (optional)**
Salt and pepper	
Fresh bread- crumbs (optional)	**French dressing**

GARNISH

1 hard-boiled egg	**Parsley**

Pick the crab meat from the shells. Mix the dark crab meat with salt and pepper, fresh breadcrumbs and a little lemon juice if liked. The breadcrumbs are optional but they lessen the richness and give a firmer texture. Press the mixture lightly against the sides of the previously cleaned shell. Flake up the white meat, mix with French dressing and pile in the centre of the shell. Garnish with sieved egg yolk, chopped egg white, chopped parsley, sieved coral if any, and decorate with small claws. Make a necklace with the small claws, place on a dish and rest the crab on this. Surround with salad.

4 helpings

CUCUMBER CREAM SOUP

1 lb cucumber	**Green colouring**
1 oz butter	**A sprig of mint**
6 spring onions	**A sprig of parsley**
1 oz flour	**⅛ pt cream**
1 pt white stock	
Salt and pepper	
Lemon juice	

Peel the cucumber, reserve a 2-in length for garnish, slice the rest. Melt the butter in a deep pan and cook the onions gently, without browning for 10 min. Stir in the flour, then the stock and bring to boiling point. Add the sliced cucumber and cook till tender. Sieve through a nylon sieve. Season and add lemon juice to taste. Cut the 2-in piece of cucumber into ¼-in dice and boil these in a little stock or water till just tender and add them to the finished soup. Five minutes before serving the soup add the mint and parsley. Tint the soup pale green. Stir the cream into the hot soup immediately before serving.

4 helpings   *Cooking time—20–30 min*

Seafood chowder

BORTSCH, POLISH or RUSSIAN BEETROOT SOUP

4 raw beetroots	**Shredded white**
1 qt brown stock	**leek, cabbage,**
1 onion stuck with	**beetroot, celery**
1 clove	**to make ½ pt**
Bunch of herbs	**in all**
A few caraway	**Salt and pepper**
seeds	**Grated nutmeg**
1 oz goose fat *or*	**¼ pt sour cream**
bacon fat	*or* **natural**
	yoghourt

Slice 3 of the beetroots and simmer them in the stock with the onion, clove, herbs and caraway seeds for about 1 hr or until the colour has run into the soup and the flavour is no longer raw. Melt the fat and in it cook the shreds of vegetable and the finely-grated 4th beetroot very gently for 10–15 min. Strain the stock and press the juice out of the beetroots into it. Add the shreds of vegetable and finish cooking them in the soup. Season, add a trace of nutmeg to the soup. Beat the sour cream or yoghourt into the hot soup but do not allow it to boil; *or* put a spoonful of yoghourt or sour cream into each soup plate before pouring in the soup.

6 helpings   *Cooking time—1½ hr*

SEA-FOOD CHOWDER

1 smoked haddock	**1 tablesp flour**
(1–1¼ lb)	**3–4 tablesp cream**
1–2 sliced onions	**Salt and pepper**
1 breakfastcup	**½ pt shelled**
diced raw	**prawns** *or*
potatoes	**shrimps**
2–3 skinned	**8 oz peas—**
tomatoes	**canned** *or* **frozen**
1–1½ oz butter *or*	**and cooked**
margarine	**1 dessertsp**
	freshly-chopped
	parsley

Cover the well-washed haddock with cold water, bring slowly to boil then remove and wash again. Skim off scum from the stock. Cook onions in a little of the stock until almost soft. Add potatoes and cook until soft. Cut tomatoes into eighths, discard seeds; simmer in remaining stock. Add tomatoes to other vegetables and cook a little. Meanwhile, free the haddock flesh of skin and bones. Melt the fat, add flour and cook for a few min without browning. Remove from heat. Slowly stir the strained remaining stock into this roux. Cook gently for a few min, while stirring. Stir in the cream and season to taste. Add the vegetable mixture, then the haddock and prawns or shrimps, reserving a few. Add the drained peas. Heat through but do not boil. Sprinkle in the parsley, turn into a serving dish and garnish with the reserved shellfish.

4-5 helpings

FRIED WHITEBAIT
Whitebait is seasonable from February to July

Whitebait	**Cayenne** *or* **black**
Ice	**pepper**
Flour	**Salt**
Deep fat for frying	**Lemon**

Frying whitebait is a difficult task for inexperienced cooks. The following is a well-tried method which, if carefully followed, usually produces satisfactory results. Put the whitebait with a piece of ice in a basin, which must be kept cool. When required for cooking, spread the fish on a cloth to dry, dredge well with flour, place in a wire basket and shake off the superfluous flour. Plunge the basket into a pan of clean, very hot lard and fry rapidly for 3–4 min. Keep moving the basket all the time while frying. Lift the basket, shake it to strain off the fat, and turn the fish on to greaseproof paper. Place on a warm dish and repeat until all the whitebait are fried. Season with cayenne or black pepper and fine salt. Serve garnished with quarters of lemon.

COQUILLES OF COOKED HALIBUT or TURBOT

½ pt white sauce	**Grated cheese**
¾ lb cooked	**Browned**
halibut *or* **turbot**	**breadcrumbs**
	Salt and pepper
	Butter

flavour the sauce with grated cheese to taste. Divide the fish into large flakes, put into 6 buttered scallop shells, cover with sauce and sprinkle thickly with browned breadcrumbs. Season, put 1 or 2 small pieces of butter on each, cook for 15–20 min in a moderate oven (180 °C, 350 °F, Gas 4).

6 helpings

MUSSELS—CHOOSING AND PREPARING

Mussels are bought while still alive and their shells should be tightly shut. Discard any that do not shut immediately when given a sharp tap, as they are probably dead. Mussels are in season from September to March. They can be served cold with vinegar or hot in soups, sauces or pies. To prepare mussels, allow 1–1½ pt mussels per person. Scrape and clean the shells thoroughly in several lots of cold water. Mussels are not opened with a knife like oysters, but open themselves during cooking. The only part of a mussel which needs to be removed is the breathing apparatus which is found in the form of a black strip known as the 'beard'. This is removed after the shells have been opened.

There are two simple methods of opening mussels:

English method

For a small quantity of 1–2 pt, place the mussels (after cleaning) in a rinsed wide pan and cover them closely with a folded damp teacloth. Heat quickly, shaking the pan at intervals, and at the end of 5–7 min the shells will open. Remove from the heat promptly as overcooking toughens them.

French method

To 3½ pt of cleaned mussels in a wide pan, add 1 shallot, finely chopped, 5–6 stalks of parsley, a sprig of thyme, ⅓ of a bay leaf, a pinch of pepper and ¼ pt dry white wine (½ water and ½ dry cider can be used). Cover the pan tightly and cook over a sharp heat for 5–6 min, shaking the pan from time to time. Remove from the heat as soon as the shells open.

MUSSELS FLORENTINE

12 fresh or	1 oz flour
canned mussels	½ pt milk
12 oz spinach	Seasoning
1½ oz butter	A little grated cheese

Cook the spinach. Put the shellfish in a small saucepan and add their liquor, previously strained through muslin. Poach for 2–3 min until the edges just begin to ruffle slightly, then remove from the heat. Melt the butter in a saucepan, stir in the flour and cook for 2 min. Add the milk, stir until boiling and boil for 3 min. Cool slightly, then add the shellfish and their liquor. Drain the spinach and spread over the bottom of a fireproof dish, pour the sauce on top, sprinkle with finely grated cheese and brown lightly under the grill. Serve immediately.

2–3 helpings

MOULES MARINIÈRES

3½ pt mussels	¼ pt dry white
1 shallot, chopped	wine (½ water
finely	and ½ dry cider
5–6 stalks of	can be used)
parsley	1 oz butter
⅓ of a bay leaf	Chopped parsley
Sprig of thyme	
Pinch of pepper	

Open the mussels by the French method. Strain the liquid through muslin, to remove any traces of sand, then return the liquid to the pan with the butter and boil rapidly until reduced by half. Meanwhile, remove the beards from the mussels, and return the mussels to their half shell, discard empty shells. Arrange in soup plates, pour the reduced liquor over the mussels and sprinkle with chopped parsley.

TROUT MEUNIÈRE

4 large *or* 8 small	A little seasoned
trout	flour
1 tablesp lemon	3 oz butter
juice	1 level tablesp
Lemon 'butterflies'	chopped parsley

Mussels Florentine

Lamb kebabs

Dredge the trout lightly, but thoroughly, with seasoned flour. Heat the butter in a frying-pan and when hot fry the trout until golden-brown and cooked through. Arrange the trout on a hot dish. Reheat the fat until it is nut-brown in colour and then pour it over the fish. Sprinkle the lemon juice and parsley over the fish, garnish with lemon 'butterflies' and serve at once.

4 helpings

FILLETS OF SOLE WITH CREAM SAUCE

1 large sole	**1 pt milk** *or* **milk**
Salt and pepper	**and fish stock**
Lemon juice	**2 oz butter**
1 small piece of	**1½ oz flour**
onion	**Parsley to**
¼ teasp ground	**garnish**
mace	**2 tablesp cream**

Wash, skin and fillet the sole, and divide each fillet lengthwise into two. Tie each strip loosely in a knot, or fold the ends over each other. Place in a greased tin, seasoned with salt and pepper, sprinkle with lemon

juice, cover with a greased paper and bake for 10–15 min in a moderate oven (180 °C, 350 °F, Gas 4). Simmer the bones of the fish, the onion and mace in the milk for about 15 min, then strain and season to taste. Melt the butter in a saucepan, add the flour, cook for 3–4 min, then pour in the flavoured milk and stir until boiling. Let the sauce simmer for 10 min at least, then add cream; arrange the fish fillets on a hot dish, either in a circle or forming 2 rows, and strain the sauce over. Decorate with a little chopped parsley.

4 helpings

SOLE À LA PORTUGAISE

1 medium-sized	**1 onion**
sole	**2–3 tomatoes**
1 oz butter	**1 dessertsp**
1 shallot	**grated Parmesan**
1 teasp finely	**cheese**
chopped parsley	**1 dessertsp**
½ teasp anchovy	**browned**
essence	**breadcrumbs**
Salt and pepper	**Extra butter**

Lamb cutlets en papillotes

Skin the sole and make an incision down the centre as for filleting; raise the flesh from the bone on each side as far as possible. Mix the butter, finely chopped shallot, parsley and anchovy essence well together, and stuff the mixture inside the sole. Place the fish in a buttered fireproof dish, season. Arrange slices of onion and tomato alternately and overlapping each other, on top of the fish; or if less onion is preferred, surround each slice of tomato with a single ring of onion. Mix together the cheese and breadcrumbs and sprinkle over the fish. Place small pieces of butter on top, cover with lid or greased paper, and bake for about 20 min in a moderate oven (180 °C, 350 °F, Gas 4).

Fillets of sole can be laid on a bed of the

stuffing and cooked in the same way. Omit the onion and tomato rings if desired.

2 helpings

SALMON CUTLETS MORNAY

2 slices of salmon	Salt and pepper
¾–1 in thick	1 oz flour
1 onion	¼ pt cream
2½ oz butter	1 tablesp grated
½ pt fish stock	Parmesan cheese
Bouquet garni	1 dessertsp
	lemon juice

Chop the onion coarsely. Melt half the butter in a shallow saucepan, fry the onion and the salmon quickly on both sides, then add the stock (boiling), the bouquet garni and salt and pepper. Cover closely, and simmer gently for 20 min. Meanwhile, melt the remainder of the butter in another saucepan, add the flour and cook 4 min. When the fish is done, transfer it to a hot dish and keep warm. Strain the stock on to the flour and butter and stir until boiling. Simmer for 5 min, then add the cream, cheese, lemon juice and seasoning to taste. Pour the mixture over the fish and serve.

DRESSED LOBSTER

Prepare the boiled lobster. Leave the meat in the shell and arrange the two halves on a bed of salad. Garnish with the claws. Serve with oil and vinegar handed separately. Piped lobster butter may be used to garnish the shell, if wished.

LOBSTER MAYONNAISE

1 boiled lobster	Salad
Mayonnaise	

Lobster Mayonnaise may be served in any of the following ways:

1 Serve like dressed lobster but with mayonnaise instead of oil and vinegar.

2 Cut the lobster in half lengthways, scoop out the meat from the body, mix with a little mayonnaise and return. Carefully remove the meat from the tail, slice and return to the shell, arranging it in overlapping slices with the red part uppermost.

Serve on a bed of salad, garnished with the claws. Serve mayonnaise separately.

3 Remove all the meat from the shell and claws. Arrange on a bed of salad, either cut into slices or roughly flaked and coa with mayonnaise.

The coral can be used, sieved, as a garnish

BEEF STROGONOFF

2 lb fillet of beef	¼ lb mushrooms
Flour	2 oz butter
Salt and pepper	A little brown
1 large onion	stock
	½ pt sour cream

Cut the beef into small very thin pieces and shake in a wire sieve with a mixture of flour, salt and pepper. Chop the onion Heat the butter in a saucepan and fry the onion until golden-brown. Add the bee and chopped mushrooms, fry a little and then moisten with the stock. Stir, and continue cooking for about 15–20 min. Pour over the sour cream, reheat and serve.

6 helpings   *Time—40 mi*

BEEF À LA MODE

2 lb rump of beef	1 oz butter *or* fat
1 glass claret	10 button onions
Juice of ½ lemon	1 oz flour
1 small onion	1½ pt stock
2 cloves	2 bacon rashers
Salt and pepper	2 carrots
Bouquet garni	

Trim and bone the meat. Place it in a bowl with a marinade made from the claret lemon juice, finely chopped onion, clove salt, pepper and bouquet garni. Leave for 2 hr, basting frequently. Melt the fat in stewpan, drain the beef well and fry unt brown. Fry the button onions at the same time. Remove both from the pan, add the flour and fry until nut-brown. Then add the stock and the marinade in which the meat was soaked and stir until boiling Replace the meat and the onions and season to taste. Cover the meat with the bacon rashers. Add the carrots, thinly sliced, and cook gently for 2½ hr, stirring occasionally When tender, place on a hot dish, strai the liquid in the saucepan and pour over the meat.

8 helpings

TOURNEDOS OF BEEF À LA NELSON

1½–2 lb fillet of beef, cut as tournedos	1 glass Madeira (optional)
¼ pt small button onions	½ pt brown *or* Espagnole sauce
Stock	⅓ pt diced potatoes
Salt and pepper	

Ask the butcher to prepare the tournedos. Parboil the onions in strong stock and then strain them. Fry the tournedos very lightly in hot fat to seal them, drain and place in individual casseroles. Season with salt and pepper and add the onions. Add the wine to the sauce, season to taste and add to the casseroles. Cook in a moderate oven (180 °C, 350 °F, Gas 4) for about 40 min. Fry the potato dice in hot fat until well browned. Drain well and add to the casseroles 10 min before serving.

6 helpings

LAMB CUTLETS EN PAPILLOTES

6 lamb cutlets	1 dessertsp chopped parsley
A few slices cooked ham	Salt and pepper
Salad oil *or* butter	Grated rind of ½ lemon
onion	
1 dessertsp chopped mushrooms	

Prepare and trim the cutlets neatly. Cut 12 small rounds of ham just large enough to cover the round part of the cutlet. Melt a little fat in a pan and fry the finely-chopped onion until tender. Add the mushroom, parsley, salt, pepper and a little grated lemon rind. Mix well and then cool. Prepare 6 heart-shaped pieces of strong white paper large enough to hold the cutlets. Grease them well with oil or butter. Place a slice of ham on one half of each paper with a little of the chopped mixture on top. Lay the cutlet on the mixture, with more of the mixture on top and place a round of ham over that. Fold over the paper and twist the edges well together. Lay the prepared cutlets in a greased baking-tin and cook for 30 min in a fairly hot oven (190 °C, 375 °F, Gas 5). Serve in the papers on a hot dish. A little good sauce may be served separately.

This method of cooking can be used with a number of different stuffings. Fried breadcrumbs mixed with chopped sautéed onions is good. So is a mixture of fresh white breadcrumbs, capers and a little garlic salt.

6 helpings   *Cooking time—about 30 min*

LAMB KEBABS

6 neat pieces of lamb, cut from leg	6 small mushrooms
3 small sliced onions	6 small tomatoes
6 thick bacon rashers	Oil *or* melted butter
	12 bay leaves

Trim the meat into neat even-shaped cubes. Cut the bacon in squares, and slice the tomatoes. Brush all (including tomatoes) with oil or butter and thread on to 6 skewers, interleaving with bay leaves. Grill for 10–15 min, turning as required. Serve on their skewers and if liked on a bed of risotto (rice cooked in stock in a casserole until stock is absorbed).

6 helpings

WIENER SCHNITZEL

6 fillets of veal about ½ in thick	1 egg
Salt and pepper	¼ lb dry breadcrumbs
1 tablesp flour	3 oz butter
	1 lemon

See that each fillet is neatly trimmed, lay on a board and beat with a cutlet bat. Sprinkle the fillets with salt and pepper. Put the flour on a plate, and lightly coat each fillet. Beat the egg and into it dip each fillet. Coat the fillets with breadcrumbs. Put the butter into a frying-pan and when hot fry the fillets on each side to a rich golden-brown. Drain and garnish with lemon.

6 helpings

JOINTING BIRDS
Top, cut legs from body, cut wing tips off.

Centre, cut breast down to wing joint, remove wing.

Bottom, split back.

BRAISED PORK CHOPS IN CIDER

4 pork chops	2–3 large dark
4 tablesp cider	mushrooms
Bouquet garni	1 breakfastcup *or*
3 onions	10-oz can garden
2 cooking apples	peas
Good pinch of	1 breakfastcup *or*
ground cinnamon	10-oz can
Salt and pepper	beetroots
	6–8 oz noodles

Trim off rind and excessive fat and quickly fry chops in them until golden-brown. Place in a casserole, add cider and bouquet garni, cover and cook gently on the cooker or in a cool oven (150°–170°C, 300°–325°F, Gas 2–3). Meanwhile, pour off excess fat from frying-pan; peel, chop, then fry the onions and apples for a few minutes. Add the cinnamon and water to cover them, put on a lid and simmer until soft. Sieve, season to taste and turn on to the chops. Cover and cook for 1¾–2 hr in all, adding the thickly sliced mushrooms ½ hr before the end. Heat the peas and beetroots separately. Trickle the noodles into salted boiling water and boil until, on testing a piece, the centre is still slightly firm (about 8 min). Drain the noodles, peas and beet-

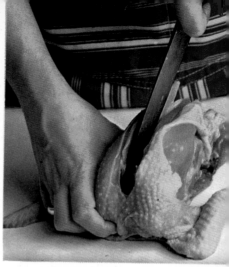

Chicken with suprême sauce.

roots. Dish the noodles with the chops on top and garnish with the mushrooms, peas and beetroots.

4 helpings

BOILED GAMMON OR BACON WITH OLIVES

Gammon or bacon joint	Black olives
Apricot jam or treacle	Chopped parsley
	Piquant sauce

Soak the gammon or bacon for at least 2 hr, changing the water at the end of 1 hr if very salt. Scrape the underside and rind as clean as possible. Put into a pan with cold water to cover. Bring to simmering point, remove any scum, then simmer for 20–25 min per lb until tender. When done, remove from the water, strip off the skin, and drain well. Spread with apricot jam or treacle, and put in a fierce oven for a few moments to glaze. Then sprinkle with chopped, stoned black olives and chopped parsley. Serve with Piquant sauce and with boiled potatoes or pease pudding.

33

KIDNEYS WITH ITALIAN SAUCE

1½ lb calves' kidneys	1 pt Italian sauce
2 oz seasoned flour	Long grained boiled rice
2 oz beef dripping	Parsley
6–8 small onions	

Prepare the kidney cutting into ½-in slices after removing skin and core. Coat the kidney well with seasoned flour. Heat the dripping in a sauté pan and fry the kidney quickly on both sides, then slowly for 10 min with a lid on the pan. Sauté the onions at the same time, and shake the pan occasionally to turn them. Drain the kidney from the fat, place in the sauce and simmer for about ¾ hr. Serve hot garnished with long grain boiled rice and parsley.

6 helpings

ROAST CHICKEN, FRENCH STYLE

1 roasting chicken	2 or 3 rashers of bacon
1 oz butter	
1 small onion	Salt and pepper
1 carrot	1½ gill chicken stock

GARNISH

Watercress

Truss the chicken for roasting, and spread the breast thickly with butter. Slice the vegetables, place them in roasting tin with bacon and the washed liver and heart of the bird; fry gently. Place the bird on the mirepoix of vegetables. Roast in a hot oven (220 °C, 425 °F, Gas 7) for 1–1½ hr until tender. Cover the breast with buttered paper if it browns too quickly; baste if necessary. When cooked, remove trussing string. Keep the chicken hot. Drain the fat from the roasting tin, add stock, boil 2–3 min, season and strain into gravy-boat. Serve with gravy, and garnished with the watercress.
Instead of the gravy, the chicken can be served with ¾ pt Italian sauce, white or brown, and with diced carrot, turnip, leek and celery, cooked for food value.

5–6 helpings

COQ AU VIN

One 3 lb cockerel or frozen roasting chicken or chicken joints	12–16 pickling onions
Stock	1 small glass brandy
¼ lb pickled belly of pork or green bacon	1 carrot
	1 onion
	1 clove garlic
6–8 oz button mushrooms, fresh or canned	Bouquet garni (2 if possible)
	Salt and pepper
2 teasp tomato purée (optional)	3 small fried croûtes per person, round or triangular, 12 in all
1½ pt red wine	Beurre manié

Joint the chicken if whole. Make a little stock from the giblets or a chicken stock cube, if necessary. Cut the pork into small cubes with extra fat if needed and fry slightly. Add the chicken pieces and fry until golden. Add the mushrooms and tomato purée if used, and the onions. Toss in the fat. Heat the brandy, set light to it and pour it over the chicken. Shake the pan, until the flames die down. Add the stock and wine, carrot, onion, garlic, bouquet and seasoning. Cover the pan and simmer gently for 40 min, or until the chicken pieces are tender. Remove the chicken and vegetables, etc., discard the carrot, onion and bouquet, and keep the rest hot in the oven, with the fried croûtes. Strain the wine sauce into a clean saucepan. Add the beurre manié in small pieces and stir until dissolved in the sauce. Simmer until the sauce is reduced to the consistency you want, but do not boil. Lay the croûtes in a hot casserole, with the chicken on top, pour the sauce over, and serve very hot.

CHICKEN WITH SUPRÊME SAUCE

1 chicken	1½ pt white stock (approx)
¾ pt Suprême sauce	

GARNISH

Macédoine of vegetables *or* **grape garnish as below**

Truss the chicken, poach it in the stock until tender, then divide into neat joints. Arrange the joints on a hot dish, pour the sauce over, and garnish with the chopped macédoine of vegetable piled at either end of the dish.

As an alternative garnish, toss 1 chopped red pepper and 1 cooked potato (sliced) in the sauce before pouring it over the chicken. Top with black and green grapes.

4–6 helpings   Cooking time—about 1½–2 hr

CURRIED CHICKEN DUCHESSE

1 boiled chicken *or*	**1 egg**
1-lb can of chicken	**Salt and pepper**
1 pt curry sauce	**Juice of 1 lemon**
½ gill cream *or* **milk**	

GARNISH

Chopped parsley	**Sippets of fried bread** *or* **creamed potato border**

Cut the chicken into joints, remove skin and excess fat. Make sauce, thoroughly heat chicken in it, add cream and egg, stir over a low heat until the sauce thickens but do not boil. Season, add lemon juice. Arrange chicken in an entrée dish, strain sauce over and garnish.

If a potato border is used, pipe or fork this into the dish, before arranging the chicken for serving.

6 helpings   Cooking—time 20 min (excluding sauce)

CURRY SAUCE, MILD

1 medium-sized onion	**½ pt pale stock, coconut infusion**
1 oz butter *or* **margarine**	**(see below)** *or* **water**
1 small cooking apple	**½ teasp black treacle**
¼–½ oz curry powder	**1–2 teasp lemon juice**
½ oz rice flour *or* **flour**	**1 dessertsp chutney**
	Salt

Chop the onion, put it into a saucepan and fry it very gently in the butter for 10 min. Chop the apple and cook it in the butter with the onion for a further 10 min. Stir in the curry powder and heat it for a few minutes. Add the flour and then stir in the liquid. When boiling, add all the other ingredients and simmer the sauce for at least ½ hr, or better 1½ hr.

To make the coconut infusion Soak 1 oz desiccated *or* fresh grated coconut in ½ pt water for a few minutes, bring slowly to boiling point and infuse it for 10 min. Wring the coconut in a piece of muslin to extract all the liquid.

STUFFED DUCKLING

1 large 4–5 lb duckling	**Sections of 1 large orange** *or* **apple**
Fat for basting	**and sauerkraut dressing**
¾ pt brown sauce	

STUFFING

1 chicken liver	**Salt and pepper**
1 duckling liver	**Nutmeg**
½ teasp parsley	**1 oz butter**
¼ teasp thyme	**1 egg**
3 oz breadcrumbs	

Blanch chicken and duckling livers, chop them finely, add herbs, breadcrumbs, melted butter, pinch of nutmeg, salt and pepper. Bind this stuffing with egg. Stuff the duckling; truss, baste well with hot fat, and roast in a hot oven (220–230 °C, 425–450 °F, Gas 7–8) for ½ hr, basting frequently. Drain off all the fat, pour the hot brown sauce into the baking tin and continue cooking until the duckling is tender (about 20 min.) Baste frequently with sauce. Serve on a hot dish. Strain a little sauce round, garnish with orange sections (heated in a little wine or stock, over a pan of hot water), and serve the remainder of the sauce separately.

Serve a dressing of canned sauerkraut with cored apple slices tossed in butter instead of the orange if you wish.

4 helpings   Cooking time—1 hr

Curried chicken duchesse

BROAD BEANS WITH CREAM SAUCE

2 lb broad beans	**½ pt veal** *or*
A bunch of herbs	**chicken stock**
(thyme, sage,	**1 lump of sugar**
savory, marjoram,	**1 egg yolk**
parsley stalks *or*	**¼ pt single cream**
any one of these)	*or* **evaporated**
	milk
	Salt and pepper

Shell the beans and cook them in the stock with the lump of sugar and the bunch of herbs. When the beans are tender, lift out the herbs. Beat the egg yolk with the cream and stir it carefully into the saucepan. Re-heat, stirring all the time until almost simmering. Season and serve at once.

TWO WAYS WITH FRENCH OR RUNNER BEANS

1½ lb French *or*	**1 oz butter** *or*
runner beans	**margarine**
	Salt

Wash, top and tail and string the beans. Do not cut up French beans *or* young runner beans as they lose their flavour in cooking. For older scarlet runners, slice thinly, or, for better flavour, cut into diamonds, i.e. slice them in a slanting direction. Have ready just enough boiling salted water to cover them and cook them with the lid on the pan. When tender (15–20 min), drain and re-heat in butter or margarine. Serve immediately. For the French method of cooking, drain the cooked beans well, and shake in the pan until most of the water has evaporated. Add a little butter, parsley, lemon juice, and seasoning and shake over heat for a few minutes. Serve immediately.

4–6 helpings

COOKED MIXED VEGETABLES

1½ lb mixed vegetables:

In winter: **parsnip, turnip, carrot, leek, cauliflower**

In summer: **new carrots, new turnips, broad beans, peas, spring onions, tomato**

Broad beans with cream sauce

Braised celery

1 oz butter *or* **margarine**
Salt and pepper
Chopped parsley
½–1 gill boiling water

Prepare all the vegetables. Cut the winter vegetables into thin slices, cutting the slices in halves or quarters when large. Break the cauliflower into sprigs. Leave most of the summer vegetables whole, cutting the carrots in thick slices, if not really small, trimming the spring onions rather short and cutting the tomatoes into wedges. Melt the fat in a saucepan. Add the vegetables to it at intervals, starting with the ones which take the longest time to cook. Put the lid on the pan after each addition and toss the vegetables in the fat. (Do not add the tomatoes to the summer vegetables until 5 min before serving.) Add the liquid and the salt (use very little water with the summer vegetables), and simmer gently until the vegetables are tender. Serve hot, sprinkled with chopped parsley.

5 helpings   Cooking time—winter vegetables, about ¾ hr; summer vegetables, about ½ hr

RED CABBAGE WITH APPLES

1 small red cabbage	**1 tablesp golden syrup**
1 oz margarine	**Juice of ½ lemon**
1 onion chopped very fine	**2 tablesp vinegar**
2 cooking apples	**Salt**

Melt the fat. Add the onion and fry gently

until light brown. Add cabbage finely shredded, peeled and sliced apples, and syrup. Cook over very gentle heat for 10 min, shaking pan frequently. Add lemon juice, vinegar and salt and simmer covered, 1–1½ hr. Stir occasionally. Season and serve.

6 helpings

BROCCOLI

This vegetable is known to the cook in three different forms:
1 Most of the cauliflowers which are sold between October and June come from the broccoli plant, which is very hardy. (The cauliflower plant proper is less hardy and supplies the typical white heads during the summer and early autumn, before the frosts appear.) This form of broccoli is cooked by the methods suggested for CAULIFLOWER.
2 The Calabresse, green or Italian sprouting broccoli, produces a medium-sized green central head, and is usually available in March. It is also cooked like cauliflower and served with melted butter. After the central head is cut, shoots appear from every leaf joint, each shoot having a tiny head. The shoots are cut with about 6 in of stem and provide an excellent vegetable for two or three months. The stems should be cut into short lengths and cooked, with the tiny heads, in boiling salted water as for any green vegetable; or they can be tied in bundles and cooked and served like asparagus.

3 Early purple sprouting and white sprouting broccoli come into season at the beginning of April. The tiny heads should be cut off with about 2 in of stem and adjoining leaves and cooked whole in boiling salt water like any other green vegetable. The more the heads are cut off the more prolific is the growth.

Frozen broccoli is available most of the year. It should be short-cooked in very little water until just tender, and served with melted butter and a sprinkling of ground nutmeg or thyme.

BRAISED CELERY

| 4 heads of celery | Glaze |
| Stock | (if available) |

MIREPOIX

$\frac{1}{2}$ oz dripping	Bouquet garni
$\frac{1}{2}$ oz bacon	(thyme,
2 large carrots	marjoram, sage,
1 small turnip	parsley)
2 onions	Watercress to
	garnish
	1 bay leaf
	Salt

Trim the celery but leave the heads whole. Wash them well and tie each securely. Prepare the mirepoix. Fry the bacon in the dripping in a large saucepan, then fry all the vegetables cut in pieces $\frac{3}{4}$ in thick, until lightly browned. Add herbs, spices and $\frac{1}{2}$ teasp of salt and enough stock to come $\frac{3}{4}$ of the way up the vegetables. Bring to boiling point. Lay the celery on top. Baste well with the stock in the pan and cover closely with greased paper or metal foil. Put on lid and cook until the celery is soft (about $1\frac{1}{2}$ hr). Baste several times during cooking. Dish the celery and keep hot. Strain the liquor, put it back in the pan and add 1 teasp of glaze if available. Reduce by boiling quickly until of glazing consistency. Pour over the celery.
Note: Use the coarse outer stems of the celery for soups. A few pieces may be cut up and fried for the mirepoix. The cooked mirepoix can be served sprinkled with parsley as a separate vegetable dish or if sieved and thinned down with stock it makes an excellent soup.

4–8 helpings, according to the size of the celery heads

BOILED, MASHED OR CREAMED POTATOES

2 lb even-sized	Salt
potatoes, old *or*	Chopped parsley
new	

Scrub the potatoes. Peel or scrape thinly, if desired. Rinse and put in a saucepan with enough *boiling* water to cover, and 1 teasp salt per qt water. Boil gently for 15–40 min according to age and size. Test with a fine skewer. When cooked, drain, steam-dry for a moment over low heat, and serve hot, sprinkled with chopped parsley.
For mashed potatoes, use:

2 lb potatoes	A little milk
1 oz butter *or*	Salt and pepper
margarine	Grated nutmeg
Chopped parsley	

Prepare and cook peeled potatoes as for Boiled Potatoes, pass them through a sieve, or through a potato masher, or mash with a fork. Melt the fat (in one corner of the pan if the potatoes have been mashed in the pan itself) and beat in the potatoes. Add milk gradually and beat well until the mixture is thoroughly hot, and smooth. Season well and add a little grated nutmeg. Serve in a hot dish. Sprinkle with chopped parsley.
Successful mashed potato depends upon the use of a floury type of potato, thorough drying of the potatoes after the water has been strained off them, and the thorough mashing of the potatoes before the fat and milk are added.
For creamed potatoes, add 1 tablesp cream (single or double) to mashed potatoes.

CHOCOLATE CHOUX OR PROFITEROLES

4 oz chou pastry as below
Icing sugar

FILLING

Sweetened whipped cream
¼ pt chocolate sauce

CHOU PASTRY

4 oz plain flour	**½ teasp vanilla**
½ pt water	**essence**
½ teasp salt	**1 egg yolk**
2 oz butter *or*	**2 eggs**
margarine	

Sift and warm the flour. Place water, salt and fat in a pan, and bring to boiling point. Remove from heat, add flour all at once and beat well over the heat again, until it becomes a smooth soft paste and leaves the sides of the pan clean. Remove from the heat, add vanilla and egg yolk immediately and beat well. Add the other two eggs one at a time, beating thoroughly between each addition. (It is important to get the first of the egg in while the mixture is hot enough to cook it slightly, otherwise it becomes too soft.) Add any flavouring last. Use while tepid.

Put the pastry into a forcing bag and pipe balls on to a greased baking-sheet using a 1-in pipe; or shape the mixture with a spoon into piles. Bake in a fairly hot oven (220–200 °C, 425–400 °F, Gas 7–6) for 30 min (do not open the door), then reduce the heat to 170 °C, 325 °F, Gas 3 for about 10 min until the buns are dried inside. Cover with greaseproof paper if they are becoming too brown. Split the buns and remove any damp mixture. Dry in the turned-off oven for a few moments if very damp.

For baby cream buns or choux, sometimes called profiteroles, use a teasp or small forcing pipe to shape the pastry into walnut-sized piles. Bake for 10 to 12 min at the higher heat, and a further 5–8 min at the reduced heat. Split, and dry out like cream buns if required. Do not underbake.

When the choux or profiteroles are cold, fill with sweetened whipped cream mixed with 1 tablesp chocolate sauce. Replace the tops and dust with icing sugar. Serve the rest of the sauce separately.

These baby choux are attractive among a selection of petits fours.

CHOCOLATE SAUCE

2 rounded	**3 rounded**
dessertsp cocoa	**dessertsp sugar**
1 rounded	**½ pt water**
dessertsp	**3 drops vanilla**
cornflour	**essence**
½ oz butter	

Blend together the cornflour, cocoa and sugar with a little of the water. Boil remaining water and pour on to blended mixture. Return to pan and boil for 2 min, stirring all the time. Add vanilla and butter. Serve hot or cold.

CARAMEL CUSTARD

3 oz loaf sugar	**¾ pt milk**
½ gill cold water	**A few drops of**
4 eggs	**vanilla essence**
1 oz castor sugar	

Have ready a warm charlotte or plain mould.

Prepare caramel with loaf sugar and water, by heating together without stirring, till golden-brown. Pour into mould.

Work together the eggs and sugar without beating them, and pour the warmed milk on them. Add the vanilla essence. Strain the custard into the mould, and cover with greased paper. Steam very slowly for about ¾ hr until the custard is set in the centre; or stand the custard uncovered in a tray of warm water and bake in a warm oven (170 °C, 355 °F, Gas 3) until the centre is set. This takes about 40 min. Turn the custard out carefully so that the caramel runs off and serves as a sauce. Small caramel custards can be made in dariole moulds. Cook for about 20 min.

6 helpings

STRAWBERRY SHORTCAKE

8 oz plain flour	**4½ oz margarine**
⅛ teasp salt	**2 oz sugar**
Pinch of baking-	**1 egg yolk**
powder	
½ oz ground almonds	

Fruit flan

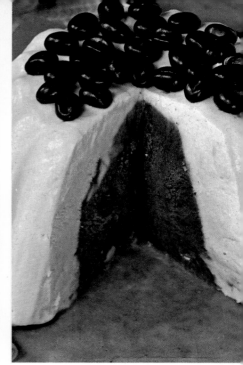

Coffee ice cream

FILLING

1 pt strawberries	**1–2 gills whipped**
Sugar to taste	**cream**

Sift flour, salt and baking-powder and mix with the ground almonds. Cream the fat and sugar and add egg yolk. Work in the flour mixture as for a cake of shortbread. Divide into three pieces and roll into rounds a good $\frac{1}{4}$ in thick. Bake in a moderate oven (180 °C, 350 °F, Gas 4) until golden-brown, then allow to become cold. Crush strawberries slightly with sugar to taste and add a little whipped cream. Spread this on to the first round of shortcake, cover with the second round and so on finishing with a layer of strawberries. Pipe whipped cream on top and round edges. Decorate as desired.

Cooking time—30–40 min

Note: Self-raising flour may be used if liked, without the baking powder. 2 Pears make a good addition to the strawberries. Slice the peeled pears, poach them and drain well before using.

CHARTREUSE OF BANANAS
(A fancy full cream)

2 pt clear lemon	**$\frac{1}{2}$ pt double cream**
jelly, as below	**Vanilla essence**
1 oz pistachio nuts	**Castor sugar to**
4 bananas	**taste**

Line a 1 qt border or ring mould with jelly. Blanch, skin, chop and dry the pistachio nuts, mix with 2 tablesp jelly and run smoothly over the base of the mould. When set, cover with a $\frac{1}{2}$-in layer of clear jelly. Slice a banana evenly, dip each slice in jelly and arrange them, slightly overlapping, in an even layer on the jelly when set. Cover with another $\frac{1}{2}$-in layer of clear jelly and allow to set. Repeat with fruit and

Pear and strawberry shortcake

jelly until the mould is full, the last layer being jelly. When set, turn out and pipe the whipped cream, sweetened, and flavoured with vanilla, into the centre. Surround with chopped jelly.

Strawberries or tangerines may be substituted for bananas and the chartreuse named accordingly.

6 helpings Setting time—(without ice) 2–3 hr; (with ice) ¾ hr

LEMON JELLY

4 lemons	1 in cinnamon
Sherry (optional)	stick
1½ pt water	1¾–2 oz gelatine
6 oz sugar	Shells and whites
4 cloves	of 2 eggs

Scald a large pan, whisk and metal jelly mould. Wash the lemons and cut thin strips of rind, omitting the white pith. Extract juice and measure. Make up to ½ pt with water *or* sherry, but do not add sherry until just before clearing the jelly. Put the 1½ pt water, ½ pt juice, rinds, sugar, flavourings and gelatine into the scalded pan and infuse, with a lid on, over very gentle heat until sugar and gelatine are dissolved. Do not let the infusion become hot. Wash egg-shells and crush. Lightly whisk the whites until liquid and add, with shells, to the infusion. Heat steadily, whisking constantly, until a good head of foam is produced, and the contents of the pan become hot, but not quite boiling. Strain through the crust as described above, and add the sherry, if used, as the jelly goes through the filter.

6 helpings *Time 1–1½ hr*

FRUIT FLAN

Rich short crust pastry or pâté sucrée, using 4 oz flour, etc.

FILLING

1 medium-sized can of fruit *or* ¾ lb fresh fruit, e.g. strawberries, pears, pineapple, cherries, apricots, peaches, etc.

COATING GLAZE

¼ pt syrup from canned fruit *or* fruit juice *or* water	**Sugar (if necessary)**
	1 teasp arrowroot
	Lemon juice to taste

DECORATION (optional)

Whipped sweetened cream

Line a 7-in flan ring with the pastry. Prick the bottom of the flan, and bake it 'blind'. Bake for about 30 min first in a fairly hot oven (200 °C, 400 °F, Gas 6) reducing the heat as the pastry sets to moderate (180 °C, 350 °F, Gas 4). When the pastry is cooked remove the paper and dummy used for blind baking and replace the case in the oven for 5 min to dry the bottom. Allow to cool.
If fresh fruit is used, stew gently till tender, if necessary. Drain the fruit. Place the sugar if used and liquid in a pan and boil for 10 min. Blend the arrowroot with some lemon juice and add it to the syrup, stirring all the time. Continue stirring, cook for 3 min then cool slightly. Arrange the fruit attractively in the flan case and coat it with fruit syrup.
If liked, the flan may be decorated with piped whipped, sweetened cream.
For a quick flan or tart case, a crumb crust or cake mixture from a packet can be used satisfactorily.

CRÈME BRÛLÉE

½ pt fresh milk	**Vanilla essence *or* brandy**
½ pt cream	**Icing sugar**
5 eggs	**Chopped, blanched almonds (optional)**
2 oz sugar	

Heat milk and cream until almost boiling. Beat eggs and sugar together to blend well. Pour on the hot milk and cream, stirring well. Add vanilla *or* brandy to taste. Strain into a 1½-pt fireproof china soufflé case. Bake very gently for approximately 1 hr in a very cool oven. Use a water bath if oven is hotter than 130 °C, 265 °F, Gas ½. When set, allow to cool and dredge the surface to a depth of ⅛ in with icing sugar. Sprinkle chopped almonds over lightly if liked. Grill until sugar has been changed to caramel.
Serve cold, with whipped cream.
Note: This recipe may be varied by substituting 1 pt cream for ½ pt fresh milk and ½ pt cream, and using 8 egg yolks instead of 5 whole eggs. Proceed as above.
6 helpings

SAVARIN

4 oz plain flour	**1 egg**
Pinch of salt	**¼ oz sugar**
¼ oz yeast	**1½ oz butter**
¼ gill warm water	

KIRSCH SAUCE

3 oz loaf sugar	**1–2 tablesp kirsch**
¼ pt water	**Juice of ½ lemon**

DECORATION

Apricot jam	**Blanched almonds, browned**

Sift the flour and salt into a basin and put it to warm. Cream the yeast with the tepid water. Make a well in the centre of the flour and pour in the yeast mixture. Sprinkle over the top with a little of the flour from the side of the bowl. Leave to prove for 10–15 min in a warm place. Add the egg gradually, beating well to a smooth elastic dough, using a little more tepid water if necessary. Knead well. Put the dough back into the basin and press down, sprinkle the sugar on the top and put on the butter in small pieces. Cover with a damp cloth and leave in a warm place to double its size. Beat well again until all the sugar and butter is absorbed. Grease a border mould and fill it ⅓ of the way up with the mixture.

Leave to prove in a warm place until the mixture just reaches the top of the mould. Then bake in a fairly hot oven (200 °C, 400 °F, Gas 6) for about 20 min.
Make the sauce: boil the water and sugar steadily for about 10 min. Add the kirsch and the lemon juice.
Turn the savarin out on to a hot dish, prick with a needle or hatpin and soak well in the sauce. Coat with hot sieved apricot jam and decorate with spikes of almonds, etc. Serve with the rest of the sauce poured round.
A savarin can be served with a rum sauce. Use rum instead of kirsch. It can also be served, hot or cold with stewed cherries and stiffly-whipped sweetened cream in the centre. In this case, make the syrup with cherry brandy. Stiffly-whipped sweetened cream mixed with crushed macaroons is another classic filling.

4 helpings

CUSTARDS FOR ICE CREAM

BASIC CUSTARD WITH EGGS

1 pt milk	4 oz castor sugar
3 eggs	

Heat the milk. Beat together the eggs and sugar. Add the hot milk slowly, stirring continuously. Return to the pan and cook without boiling until custard coats the back of a wooden spoon. Strain, cover and cool.

RICH CUSTARD

1 pt milk	2 eggs
8 egg yolks	4 oz castor sugar

Heat the milk. Beat together eggs and sugar until thick and white; add the milk. Cook, without boiling, until it thickens. Strain, cover and cool.

BASIC ICE CREAM (VANILLA)

½ pt cream	1 teasp vanilla
¼ pt cold ice cream custard	2 oz castor sugar

Half whip the cream. Add the custard, vanilla and sugar. Chill and freeze.

CHOCOLATE ICE CREAM

4 oz plain chocolate	1 gill cream
½ gill water	1–2 teasp vanilla essence
½ pt custard	

Break chocolate roughly, place in pan, add water. Dissolve over low heat. Add melted chocolate to the custard. Cool. Add the half-whipped cream and vanilla to taste. Chill and freeze.

6–8 helpings

RASPBERRY OR STRAWBERRY ICE CREAM

1 small can raspberries or strawberries	¼ pt basic custard with eggs, cold
¼ pt cream	2 oz castor sugar

Drain the fruit, and pass through a nylon sieve. The fruit and juice together should make ½ pt. Mix with the custard. Half-whip the cream and blend the two mixtures gradually. Add the sugar and a little food colouring if you wish. Chill, then freeze.

COFFEE ICE CREAM

½ pt cream	2 tablesp liquid coffee
½ pt basic custard with eggs	2 oz castor sugar

Make like the basic vanilla ice cream.

MOULDING ICES

If the mixture is to be moulded it should be removed from the freezer or fridge in a semi-solid condition, and then packed into a dry mould, well shaken, and pressed down into the shape of the mould. The mould should have a tightly-fitting lid. It should be wrapped in greaseproof paper anb buried in broken ice and freezing salt for 1½–2 hr.
To unmould, remove the paper, wipe the mould carefully, dip it into cold water, and turn the ice on to a dish in the same way as a jelly.

The Wedding

WEDDING BREAKFAST may be a formal ncheon or dinner party, with the Wedng Cake as the *piéce de rèsistance*. In is case, the hostess chooses light but emorable dishes for her menu, taking parular care that they suit the champagne d other light wines which are almost ways served.

ery often, however, the traditional wedd-g breakfast gives place to a buffet-style al, the type depending on the time of y the wedding takes place. A morning dding may be followed by cocktail-style acks; an afternoon buffet may consist of -time dainties, or may be cocktail fare er in the day. No matter what the style, wever, the focus of the buffet is always e cake', and all other food is supplemen-ry to its white glory. It should be placed the centre of the buffet or on a separate le where the bride and groom can cut it sily, and from which it can be distributed trays, ready and waiting beforehand.

in the case of a formal wedding break- t, all the other food should suit the ampagne which is usually the principal ne.

ee-tier wedding cake

WEDDING CAKE

Note: These quantities are sufficient for a 3-tier cake.

3–3¼ lb flour	24 large eggs
¼ teasp salt	5½ lb currants
3 level teasp ground cinnamon	2 lb sultanas
3 level teasp ground mace	1–1½ lb glacé cherries
1 nutmeg (grated)	1–1¼ lb mixed chopped peel
1½ teasp baking-powder	Rind and juice of 1 lemon
3 lb butter	½–1 lb blanched chopped almonds
3 lb caster sugar	1½ gills rum *or*
1½ teasp gravy browning	brandy *or* rum and brandy

Prepare and line 3 cake-tins, one 12 in diameter, one 8 in, and one 4 in diameter. Sift together flour, salt, spices and baking-powder. Mix together all the fruit with a little of the measured flour. Cream the butter and sugar very well, add browning. Add egg and flour alternately to the creamed fat beating well between each addition. Stir in the prepared fruit, almonds and brandy. Divide ½ of the mixture between the 2 smaller tins, and put the remaining ½ of the mixture in the biggest tin. Tie a thick band of brown paper round the outside of each tin. Smooth the mixture and make a depression in the centre of each cake. Bake the 4-in cake for 2–3 hr, the 8-in cake for 3½–4 hr, and the 12-in cake for 5–6 hr. Put in a cool oven (150 °C, 310 °F, Gas 2) for the first ½ hr, then reduce heat to very cool (140–130 °C, 275–250 °F, Gas 1–½) for the remainder of the time.

To cover the 4-in cake with almond paste 1 lb ground almonds, etc, will be required; 2 lb ground almonds, etc, for the 8-in cake and 3 lb ground almonds, etc, for the 12-in cake.

For the royal icing use 1 lb icing sugar, etc, for the 4-in cake, 2 lb for the 8-in cake and 3 lb sugar, etc, for the 12-in cake.

Decoration of each cake is then completed upon silver boards (of correct size) covered with a lace d'oyley. The cake is then assembled by placing one cake on top of the other with pillars supporting them. The pillars for the bottom tier should be 3 in in height and for the top the pillars should be 4 in high. Place a silver vase containing white flowers on top.

ALMOND PASTE (ICING)

Almond paste—often called almond icing or marzipan—is used to cover rich cakes before applying royal or glacé icing. (It is also used alone to decorate cakes, e.g. Simnel Cake and Battenburg Cake.) It is often coloured and flavoured and then moulded into various shapes to be used for cake decoration.

6 oz icing sugar and 6 oz castor sugar or 12 oz icing sugar	¾ teasp orange flower water ¾ teasp vanilla essence
12 oz ground almonds Juice of ½ lemon	1–2 egg yolks

Sieve the icing sugar into a bowl and mix with the ground almonds and castor sugar. Add the lemon juice, essences and enough egg yolk to bind the ingredients into a pliable but dry paste. Knead thoroughly with the hand until smooth.

Note: A whole egg or egg whites may be used instead of egg yolks. Egg yolk gives a richer and yellower paste, whilst egg white

gives a whiter, more brittle paste. (Economically the yolks can be used for almond paste and the whites used for royal icing.) This quantity of paste is sufficient to cover the top and sides of an 8-in cake.

To Apply Almond Paste

To cover the top and sides of a rich fruit cake, the cake top should be fairly level and the surface free from loose crumbs.

Brush the top and sides with warm apricot glaze, using a pastry brush. Dredge a little castor sugar on to a clean board and roll out the almond paste to a round which is 4 in wider than the diameter of the cake. Place the cake in the centre of this with its glazed top downwards and work the paste upwards round the sides of the cake with the hands until it is within ¼ in of the top edge, i.e. on the cake bottom. Using a straight-sided jar or thick tumbler, roll firmly round the sides, pressing slightly with the other hand on the upturned bottom of the cake and turning the cake round on the sugared board when necessary.

Continue rolling and turning until the sides are straight and smoothly covered and the top edges of the cake are sharp and smooth when the process is completed and the cake is turned upright.

Note: Allow a few days for the almond paste to dry, before putting on the royal icing, or the oil from the almond paste will discolour it. Cover with a clean cloth to protect from dust whilst drying.

APRICOT GLAZE

2 tablesp apricot jam	1 tablesp water

Sieve the jam and water into a saucepan. Place over heat and bring to boiling point. Remove and cool. Use to glaze the tops of small cakes, to stick almond paste to Christmas cakes, etc.

ROYAL ICING

1 lb icing sugar (approx)	2 egg whites 1 teasp lemon juice

If the sugar is lumpy, roll with a rolling-pin before sieving. Put the egg whites into bowl, beat slightly with a wooden spoon. Add 2 teasp sieved sugar and beat again. Gradually add the remainder of the sugar, beating well until a thick, smooth consistency and a good white colour are obtained. Add the lemon juice and beat again.

If a softer icing is required 1 teasp glycerine may be stirred in after the sugar; this prevents the icing becoming brittle and facilitates cutting.

If the icing is not wanted at once, cover the bowl with a damp cloth to keep it soft.

TO ICE A CAKE WITH ROYAL ICING

Place the cake, already covered with almond paste, on a cake-board or inverted plate. Place the cake-board on a turntable if available.

For an 8-in cake, use:

First coating Royal icing, using $1\frac{1}{4}$ lb icing sugar, etc, mixed to a stiff consistency.

Second coating $\frac{3}{4}$–1 lb icing sugar, etc, consistency to coat the back of a spoon.

Decorative piping $\frac{1}{2}$ lb icing sugar, etc, mixed to a stiff consistency, ie that will stand up in points when the back of the spoon is drawn away from the side of the bowl.

To Apply First Coating

With a tablesp take enough icing to cover the top, and place it in the centre of the cake. Spread evenly over top, smoothing the surface with a hot, wet palette knife (shake or dry the knife after dipping it in hot water as too much water softens the icing). Take up small portions of the icing with the end of the palette knife blade, spread it smoothly round the side until the cake is completely covered and the surface smooth.

Allow to set for a few days before applying the second coat. Whilst the icing is drying and as soon as it is hard enough, place a thin sheet of paper lightly over the top to protect it from dust.

To Apply Second Coating

Mix icing to a thin coating consistency and pour over the cake. Prick any bubbles with a fine skewer or pin; allow to firm before decorating.

Icing syringes are made of metal or plastic and can be bought in sets complete with decorative pipes. Excellent plastic turntables are also available. If coloured icings are being used the syringe must be washed before filling with another colour. All pipes must be kept clean. Always keep the bowl containing the icing covered with a damp cloth whilst decorating, to prevent the icing drying out.

The beginner should practise on an up-turned cake-tin or plate before starting on the cake, and the icing may be removed if scraped off immediately and returned to the covered bowl.

For Christmas cakes other decorations may be made with coloured marzipan, e.g. holly, marzipan, apples, etc, and the smooth icing surface roughened into points with a palette knife to form 'snow drifts'. For this one coat only is needed.

Christmas and Other Traditional Festivities

HERE ARE dishes which make a good Christmas dinner in truly traditional style. They are followed by menus which could be used by a small family or just two people. They are also suitable as Easter lunch or dinner menus.

All the recipes for these festivity menus are in this book. The section on *Dishes for Dinner Parties* above all will give the hostess ideas for other festivity meals.

After the menus, you will find recipes and suggestions for various cakes for special occasions.

TUNA SALAD IN GRAPEFRUIT

Allow one grapefruit for two helpings. Cut across in half and remove the pulp. Add to it an equal amount of drained canned peas and half this amount in flaked tuna fish moistened with mayonnaise. Cut out the core and skinny bits of the grapefruit and squeeze their juice into the grapefruit shells. Line the inside of the shells with shredded lettuce, heap the mixture into them and sprinkle with paprika.

MELON

There are various kinds of melon. They must not be over-ripe, and should be served as fresh as possible and above all, very cold.

Put crushed ice round the dish on which the slices of melon are served. Serve with powdered ginger and caster sugar.

TOMATO SOUP

1 lb tomatoes fresh *or* canned	Grated nutmeg
1 onion	Lemon juice
1 carrot	A bunch of herbs
½ oz margarine	Minute tapioca
1 oz bacon scraps, rind *or* bone	*or* cornflour
	Salt and pepper
1 pt white stock *or* juice from canned tomatoes	Sugar
	Red colouring, if needed

Slice the tomatoes, onion and carrot. If canned tomatoes are used, strain them and make the juice up to 1 pt with stock. Melt the margarine in a deep pan and lightly fry the sliced vegetables and chopped bacon for 10 min. Boil the stock or tomato juice and add to the vegetables with the nutmeg, lemon juice and herbs and cook for ¾–1 hr. Sieve and thicken the soup with ½ oz cornflour or minute tapioca to each 1 pt soup, blended with a little cold milk, stock or water. Stir into the soup, cook till clear, season, add sugar to taste and colouring if needed.

4 helpings   *Cooking time—¾–1 hr*

Roast turkey

Tomato soup

ROAST TURKEY WITH APPLE AND RICE STUFFING

One 13-lb turkey	Gravy
Apple and rice stuffing	Chipolata sausages
2–3 rashers streaky bacon	Bread sauce *or* Apple sauce
Fat for basting	Stuffed braised onions *or* apples

APPLE AND RICE STUFFING FOR TURKEY

1 chicken stock cube	1 lb cooking apples finely grated
6 oz long grain rice	3 oz fresh white breadcrumbs
3 medium-sized onions, finely chopped	1 egg to bind

6 oz frozen peas	Butter or
Salt and pepper	margarine
4–5 oz medium fat	
soft cheese	

Dissolve the stock cube in one pt of water and bring to the boil. Add the rice and onions. Simmer gently for 10 min until all the stock has been absorbed. Stir in the peas and allow the mixture to cool. Season carefully. Mix the cheese and grated apple together, and add carefully to the rice. Sprinkle on the breadcrumbs and stir in. Add the egg to bind the mixture. (This quantity is enough to stuff a 13-lb turkey, leaving enough mixture over to make 7 or 9 forcemeat balls.) Bake the forcemeat balls separately in foil with butter or margarine to baste, for about 20 min at 170 °C, 325 °F, Gas 3.

Stuff the crop of the bird with apple and rice stuffing, as well as the body. Truss the bird for roasting. Lay the bacon rashers over the breast. Roast in a preheated hot oven (220 °C, 425 °F, Gas 7) for 15–20 min; then reduce the heat to moderate (180 °C, 350 °F. Gas 4) and baste frequently until the bird is done. The cooking time will depend on the size and quality of the bird. As a general guide, allow 15 min per lb for a bird under 14 lb in weight, 12 min per lb for one over 14 lb. About 20 min before serving, remove the bacon to let the breast brown. Crumble it and add the crumbs to the sauce if wished.

When ready, dish the bird, having removed the trussing string. Serve with gravy, chipolata sausages and bread or apple sauce. Surround it with stuffed braised onions or apples.

A young turkey or turkey poult is cooked under buttered paper instead of bacon rashers, and takes only about an hour in a hot oven (220 °C, 425 °F, Gas 7). It is usually served with thin gravy and fried bacon rolls or slices of hot boiled ham.

On a large turkey, the breast meat may dry up in a small oven before the legs are cooked through. Either cover the breast with heavy-duty aluminium foil for the whole cooking time; or remove the legs before cooking (or when the breast is ready) and cook them separately for another dish.

VARIATION

An attractive way of dealing with a frozen turkey is to season and baste it with fruit juice. In this case, it is best served with the stuffed, braised onions rather than the apples. For a 9–10 lb frozen turkey, use:

1 orange	Salt and freshly
1 large onion	ground black
1 dessert apple	pepper
2 tablesp olive oil	¼ teasp dried
	rosemary
	¼ teasp dried
	oregano

BASTING JUICE

4 oz melted butter	1 chicken stock
¼ pt dry white	cube
wine	Salt and freshly
Juice of 2 oranges	ground black
1 clove garlic,	pepper
finely chopped	

STUFFED BRAISED ONIONS

6 large onions,	1 lb full-fat
peeled and	soft cheese
parboiled	Salt and freshly
1 lb cooking	ground black
apples, peeled,	pepper
cored and finely	¼ lb frozen peas,
chopped	thawed

Fully thaw the turkey before preparing any ingredients. Mix the orange segments, chopped onion and apple, olive oil, salt and pepper and herbs. Season the inside of the bird with this mixture. Prepare the basting juice by mixing all the ingredients together. Roast the turkey in the usual way, but baste with the juice instead of with fat. While the turkey is cooking, parboil the onions, stuff them with the mixed apple, cheese, seasoning and peas, and bake them in a shallow tin under the turkey until tender.

ROAST TURKEY WITH CHESTNUTS

1 turkey	Cream or milk
2–3 lb chestnuts, dried or fresh	1–1½ lb sausage meat or 1 lb sausage stuffing
¼ pt chicken stock	2–3 slices bacon
2 oz butter	Fat for basting
1 egg	Gravy
Salt and pepper	Cranberry sauce

If fresh, slit the chestnut skins, cook them in boiling water for 15 min, drain and remove the skins. If dried, soak overnight, then simmer 15 min in fresh water.
Stew the prepared chestnuts in stock for 1 hr; drain, and then chop or sieve them, keeping a few back for garnish. Make the stuffing with the chopped chestnuts, butter (melted), egg, seasoning and cream. Fill the crop of the bird with this stuffing and the body with sausage meat or stuffing, well seasoned. Truss the bird for roasting. Cover it with bacon, and roast in a moderate oven (180 °C, 350 °F, Gas 4) until tender, basting well. Times are given in the previous recipe. Towards the end of the cooking time, remove the bacon to let the breast brown. Remove the trussing string before dishing the bird. Garnish with the reserved chestnuts, and serve with gravy and cranberry sauce.

SAUSAGE STUFFING

½ lb lean pork	Salt and pepper
2 oz breadcrumbs	Grated nutmeg to taste
½ teasp mixed fresh herbs or	The liver of the bird to be stuffed
¼ teasp dried herbs	Stock
2 small sage leaves	

Mince the pork. Chop the liver. Mix all the ingredients, using enough stock to bind the mixture. Season to taste.
Use for turkey or chicken.
Note: A good bought pork sausage meat mixed with the liver of the bird makes a quick stuffing for poultry.

BREAD SAUCE

1 large onion	2 oz dry white breadcrumbs
2 cloves	
Pinch of ground mace	½ oz butter
	Salt and pepper
1 bay leaf	2 tablesp cream (optional)
4 peppercorns	
1 allspice berry	
½ pt milk	

Put the onion and spices into the milk, bring them very slowly to boiling point. Cover the pan and infuse over a gentle heat for ½–1 hr. Strain the liquid. To it add the crumbs and butter, and season to taste. Keep the mixture just below simmering point for 20 min. Stir in the cream if used, serve the sauce at once. Serve with roast chicken or turkey.

CRANBERRY SAUCE

½ lb cranberries	Sugar to taste
¼–½ pt water	

Stew the cranberries till soft, using ¼ pt water and adding more if needed. Rub the fruit through a hair or nylon sieve. Sweeten to taste. For economy, half cranberries and half sour cooking apples make an excellent sauce. Serve with roast turkey, chicken or game.

GRAVY—for any Roast Joint except Pork, and for poultry

Dripping from the roasting tin	Water in which vegetables have been boiled or stock
Flour	
Essences from the joint or poultry	Salt and pepper

Drain most of the fat from the roasting tin, carefully saving any sediment and meat juices. Dredge into the thin film of dripping sufficient flour to absorb it all. Brown this flour slowly till of a nut-brown colour. Stir in water in which green vegetables or potatoes have been cooked, or stock, allowing ½ pt for 6 persons. Boil the gravy and season it to taste.
To obtain a brown colour without brown-

Roast goose and apples coated with cloves

ing the flour, add a few drips of gravy browning from the end of a skewer.

For giblet gravy for poultry, use chicken fat and stock made with giblets.

ROAST GOOSE

1 goose	Flour
Sage and onion stuffing	Apple sauce
	Gravy (*see* **below**)
Fat for basting	

Prepare the goose, make the stuffing and insert this in the body of the bird. Truss the goose, and prick the skin of the breast. Roast the bird in a fairly hot oven 190–200 °C, 375–400 °F, Gas 5–6) for 2½ hr or until tender. When almost cooked, dredge the breast with flour, baste with some of the hot fat and finish cooking. Remove trussing string; dish the bird. Serve with apple sauce and a gravy made with thickened beef stock. Goose giblet gravy is very rich.

8–10 helpings

APPLES, APRICOTS, ETC, WITH MEAT

Apples are often baked whole and served with goose instead of apple sauce. They are cored but not peeled, and the core holes are stuffed with a little sage stuffing or with raisins, so that the apples keep their shape. They are cooked just like sweet baked apples.

SAGE AND ONION STUFFING

¼ lb onions	2 oz breadcrumbs
4 sage leaves *or*	1 oz butter
½ teasp powdered sage	Salt and pepper
	1 egg (optional)

Slice the onions thickly, parboil them for 10 min in very little water. Scald the sage leaves. Chop both. Mash all the ingredients together and season to your taste.

APPLE SAUCE

1 lb apples	Rind and juice
2 tablesp water	of ½ lemon
½ oz butter *or* margarine	Sugar to taste

Brussels sprouts with chestnuts

Cauliflower with white sauce

Stew the apples very gently with the water, butter and lemon rind until they are pulpy. Beat them quite smooth or rub them through a hair or nylon sieve. Reheat the sauce with the lemon juice and sweeten to taste.

For Apple Raisin sauce, add ½ tablesp chopped parsley and 1 oz seedless raisins before re-heating.

BOILED BRUSSELS SPROUTS WITH CHESTNUTS

1½ lb Brussels sprouts	12 cooked chestnuts
Salt	3 oz chopped ham
1 oz butter *or* margarine (optional)	4 tablesp cream

Choose small, close, sprouts. Remove shabby outer leaves by cutting the end, then make a cross cut on the bottom of each stalk. Soak in cold water, containing 1 teasp of salt per quart, for 10 min only. Wash thoroughly under running water if possible. Choose a suitably sized pan and put in enough water to ¼ fill it only, with ½ teasp salt to 1 pt of water. When boiling, put in half the sprouts, the largest ones if variable in size, put on lid and bring quickly to boil again. Add rest of sprouts and cook until all are just tender, with the lid on the pan all the time. Drain in a colander and serve immediately in a hot vegetable dish or toss in melted butter before serving. Sprouts should be served quickly as they soon cool.

To serve with chestnuts put the sprouts, chopped chestnuts, ham and cream into a casserole, cover and re-heat gently in the oven at 180 °C, 350 °F, Gas 4.

6 helpings   *Cooking time—15 min*

CHESTNUTS AU JUS

2 lb chestnuts	1 pt good brown stock
2 cloves	
1 small onion	Cayenne pepper
1 outside stick of celery	Salt
1 bay leaf	1 dessertsp meat glaze (if available)
A pinch of mace	Fleurons of pastry

Take a sharp knife and make an incision in each chestnut, in the shell only. Put into a saucepan and cover with cold water. Bring to the boil and cook for 2 min. Drain and peel and skin them while very hot. Stick the cloves into the onion and put chestnuts, onion, celery, bay leaf and mace into the boiling stock. Season. Simmer about 1 hr until the chestnuts are tender. Strain and keep the chestnuts hot. Return stock to pan, add the meat glaze if available and reduce to a glazing consistency. Pile the chestnuts in a hot vegetable dish, pour the glaze over and decorate with fleurons of pastry.

For a purée, sieve the cooked chestnuts and add a little butter and cream to taste.

6 helpings

CAULIFLOWER WITH WHITE SAUCE

1 large cauliflower	Salt
½ pt white sauce made with ½ milk and ½ cauliflower water	

Trim off the stem and all the leaves, except the very young ones. Soak in cold water, head down, with 1 teasp salt per qt of water, for not more than 10 min. Wash well. Choose a suitably sized pan and put in enough water to ¼ fill it, with ½ teasp salt to 1 pt water. Put in cauliflower, stalk down, and cook with lid on pan until stalk and flower are tender. Lift out carefully and drain. Keep hot.

Coat the cauliflower with the sauce and serve immediately.

Note: To reduce cooking time, the cauliflower may be quartered before cooking or broken into large sprigs.

6 helpings   *Cooking time—20–25 min*

GLAZED CARROTS

1½ lb young carrots	¼ teasp salt
2 oz butter	Good stock
3 lumps sugar	Chopped parsley

Melt the butter in a saucepan. Add the scraped, whole carrots, sugar, salt and enough stock to come half-way up the carrots. Cook gently, without a lid, shaking the pan occasionally until tender. Remove the carrots and keep them hot. Boil the stock rapidly until reduced to rich glaze. Replace the carrots 2 or 3 at a time, turn them until both sides are well coated with glaze. Dish, sprinkle with chopped parsley and serve.

6 helpings   *Cooking time—about ¾ hr*

GREEN PEAS

2 lb peas	A little sugar
Salt	½ oz butter *or* margarine
Sprig of mint	

Shell the peas. Have sufficient boiling salted water to cover the peas. Add the peas, mint and sugar. Simmer gently until soft, from 10–20 min. Drain well. Re-heat with butter *or* margarine and serve in a hot vegetable dish.

If the peas must be shelled some time before cooking, put them in a basin and cover them closely with washed pea-pods.

4–6 helpings (according to yield)

ROAST POTATOES

2 lb even-sized potatoes	Salt and pepper Dripping

Peel the potatoes and cut in halves or even in quarters if very large. Parboil and strain off the water and dry the potatoes over a low heat. Put into hot dripping in a roasting tin, or in the tin containing the roast joint. Roll the potatoes in the fat and cook till tender and brown.

Cooking time, to parboil, 10 min;
to bake, 1 hr (approx)

CHRISTMAS PUDDING
(Rich, boiled)

10 oz sultanas	1 level teasp mixed spice
10 oz currants	
½ lb raisins	1 level teasp grated nutmeg
2 oz sweet almonds (skinned and chopped)	¼ lb breadcrumbs
	10 oz finely-chopped *or* shredded suet
1 level teasp ground ginger	
½ lb plain flour	6 eggs
Pinch of salt	½ gill stout
1 lb soft brown sugar	Juice of 1 orange
	1 wineglass brandy
½ lb mixed finely-chopped candied peel	½ pt milk (approx)

Grease three 1-pt pudding basins. Prepare the dried fruit; stone and chop the raisins; chop the nuts.

Sift the flour, salt, spice, ginger and nutmeg into a mixing bowl. Add the sugar, breadcrumbs, suet, fruit, nuts and candied peel. Beat the eggs well and add to them the stout, orange juice and brandy, and stir this into the dry ingredients adding enough milk to make the mixture of a soft dropping consistency. Put the mixture into prepared basins. Cover and boil steadily for 6–7 hr. Take the puddings out of the water and cover them with a clean dry cloth and, when cold, store in a cool place until required.

When required, boil the puddings for $1\frac{1}{2}$ hr before serving. Serve with brandy butter.

3 puddings (each to give 6 medium helpings)

BRANDY OR RUM SAUCE

$\frac{1}{4}$ pt single cream	1 dessertsp
2 egg yolks	brown sugar
	$\frac{1}{8}$ pt brandy *or*
	2 tablesp rum

Mix all the ingredients in a basin. Set the basin over a saucepan of hot water, and whisk until the mixture thickens.
Rum sauce can also be made like Brandy Butter.

BRANDY BUTTER (Hard sauce)

3 oz butter	1 teasp–1 tablesp
6 oz icing sugar *or*	brandy
$4\frac{1}{2}$ oz icing sugar and 1 oz ground almonds	1 whipped egg white (optional)

Cream the butter till soft. Sift the icing sugar and cream it with the butter till white and light in texture. Mix in the almonds if used. Work the brandy carefully into the mixture. Fold the stiffly whipped egg white into the sauce. Serve with Christmas or other steamed puddings. This sauce may be stored for several weeks in an air-tight jar. It makes an excellent filling for sweet sandwiches.

FRUIT SALAD

3 oz granulated sugar	6 oz green grapes
$\frac{1}{2}$ pt water	1 small can pineapple segments
3 oranges	3 red-skinned dessert apples
Rind and juice of 1 lemon	
3 ripe dessert pears	

Bring the sugar and water to the boil, together with strips of rind taken from 1 orange and the lemon. Cool. Sieve to remove the rind.
Cut up the oranges, removing the skin and white pith, and section out the flesh, removing the pips. Halve the grapes, removing the pips. Place these in the cooled sugar and water. Empty the pineapple pieces and juice into the fruit salad. Refrigerate if possible.
Just before serving, quarter, core and slice the apples thinly and toss in the lemon juice. Dice the pears and also toss in lemon juice. Add these to the fruit salad. Arrange attractively in a suitable serving dish. Chill and serve.
Fresh pineapple and canned mandarin segments are attractively coloured fruit to use. Try piling the salad in a shell or half shell of pineapple. Serve with fresh cream.

MINCE PIES

Short crust, rich short crust, rough puff *or* puff pastry using 6 oz flour, etc	10–12 oz mincemeat
	Castor *or* icing sugar

Roll the pastry out to about $\frac{1}{8}$ in thickness. Cut half of it into rounds of about $2\frac{1}{2}$ in diameter and reserve these for lids. (Use a plain cutter for flaky, rough puff or puff pastry.) Cut the remaining pastry into rounds of about 3 in diameter and line some patty-tins. Place some mincemeat in the tins, brush the edge of the pastry with water and place a lid on top of each. Press the edges well together; if a plain cutter has been used knock up the edges. Brush the tops with water and sprinkle with sugar. Make a hole or 2 small cuts in the top of

Christmas cake

mincer. Add the other ingredients and mix well. Cover in jars and use as required.
Note: If the mincemeat is to be used within a few days the brandy may be omitted.

CHRISTMAS CAKE

8 oz butter *or* margarine	5–6 eggs
8 oz castor sugar	1 lb currants
½ teasp gravy browning	8 oz raisins
8 oz plain flour	4 oz glacé cherries
⅛ teasp salt	2 oz chopped peel
1 level teasp mixed spice	4 oz blanched, chopped almonds
½ level teasp baking-powder	Milk, if necessary
	4–5 teasp brandy (optional)

Line an 8-in cake-tin with greaseproof paper.
Cream the fat and sugar until white; add gravy browning. Sift together flour, salt, mixed spice and baking-powder. Add egg and flour alternately to the creamed fat, beating well between each addition. Stir in the prepared fruit, almonds and (if necessary) add a little milk to make a heavy dropping consistency. Place the mixture in the cake-tin and tie a piece of paper round the outside of the tin. Smooth the mixture and make a depression in the centre. Bake in a warm oven (170 °C, 335 °F, Gas 3) for ½ hr, then reduce heat to 150 °C, 290 °F, Gas 1 for a further 3–3½ hr. Allow to firm before removing from tin and when cold remove paper. Prick bottom of cake well and sprinkle brandy over it. Leave for a few days before icing.

Cooking time 4 hr

each. Bake in a hot oven (230–220 °C, 450–425 °F, Gas 8–7) depending on the type of pastry, for 25–30 min. Dredge tops with castor sugar *or* icing sugar. Serve hot or cold.

8–10 pies

MINCEMEAT

1¼ lb cooking apples (prepared weight)	1 level teasp ground nutmeg
1 lb currants	¼ level teasp ground cloves
1 lb seedless raisins	¼ level teasp ground cinnamon
½ lb sultanas	½ level teasp salt
¼ lb candied peel	⅛ pt brandy (*see* below)
1 lb beef suet	
1 lb sugar	
Grated rind and juice of 2 lemons *or* 1 orange and 1 lemon	

Peel and core the apples. Put these with the fruit, candied peel and suet through the

PETITS FOURS (1)

2 egg whites	Rice paper
4 oz ground almonds	Glacé cherries
2 oz castor sugar	Angelica
A few drops almond essence	

Whisk the egg whites very stiffly, and fold in gradually the mixed almonds and sugar. Drip in the almond essence as you work.

Place the mixture in a forcing bag with a large decorative pipe and force it on to rice paper in rosettes or oblongs. Decorate with tiny pieces of glacé cherry or angelica and bake in a moderate oven (180 °C, 350 °F, Gas 4) until golden-brown. They take about 20 min.

20–30 small petits fours

PETITS FOURS (2)

1 square *or* **oblong Genoese cake, 1–1½ in thick Apricot marmalade** *or* **glaze**	**Butter icing and cake crumbs Almond paste Glacé** *or* **royal icing**

Cut neat shapes from the pastry: make squares, rings, triangles and so on. Using apricot marmalade, fasten a small piece of almond paste *or* butter icing mixed with cake crumbs on top of each piece of Genoese. Coat with icing, and decorate with fine piping in scrolls etc, as you fancy.

GENOESE CAKE

4 oz flour Pinch of salt	**4 eggs 4 oz castor sugar 3 oz butter** *or* **margarine**

Sift flour and salt. Beat eggs and sugar in a basin over a pan of hot water till thick. Clarify the fat and fold lightly into egg mixture, then fold in salted flour. Pour into lined Swiss roll tin and bake in a moderate oven (180 °C, 350 °F, Gas 4). When cold (after 24 hr) cut and use as desired for small iced cakes, etc.

Cooking time—30–40 min

FESTIVITY MENUS

The dishes above provide ideas for several different Christmas menus. Here is an alternative menu for a small family or for two people, which is also suitable as an Easter menu for a family. All the recipes are in this book, for this and the following two festivity menus.

For other kinds of festivity parties, such as a Guy Fawkes outdoor party or a New Year's Eve party, pick ideas from other sections, and use the ideas for traditional cakes at the end of this section.

CHRISTMAS OR EASTER MENU

Consommé Madrilène

*

Roast Chicken, French Style
Potato Straws   Green Peas
Tomato Salad

*

Bread Sauce   Gravy

*

Tangerine Pancakes

*

Coffee

Note: Use these pancakes for a Shrove Tuesday dinner too.

EASTER OR OTHER FESTIVAL MENU

Grapefruit Baskets

*

Crown Roast of Lamb with Saffron Rice
Steamed Cucumber   Cooked Cauliflower
with White Sauce   Salad

*

Lemon or Orange Sorbet
Eastertide Biscuits

*

Coffee
Peppermint Creams

A WINTER FESTIVITY DINNER

Cucumber Cream Soup

*

Tournedos of Beef à la Nelson
Sautéed Potatoes   Stuffed Tomatoes
Boiled French Beans   Gravy
Mixed Vegetable Salad

*

Crème Brulée

*

Cheese and Biscuits

*

Coffee   Petits Fours

SPECIAL FESTIVAL CAKES

Here are ideas for cakes which you can use on various party occasions, and for some traditional festivals. Some of these cakes have a long history, and a place in the folk lore of many peoples. Gingerbreads, for instance, have been offered at festivals and fairs since pagan times, and are associated with many saints' days.

CHRISTENING CAKE

Make one of the recipes for Birthday Cake, and decorate it with almond paste and white icing. Pipe stars or rosettes round the top edge, using pink or blue icing according to whether the baby is a girl or boy. Pipe the baby's name in the centre of the cake, in the appropriate colour.

CROWN CELEBRATION CAKE

Recipe for Basic Victoria Sandwich Cake Almond paste, using 4 oz ground almonds Apricot glaze	Orange glacé icing Glacé cherries, mimosa balls, etc, to decorate

Bake the Victoria Sandwich Cake in a single 8-in ring mould, for 30–40 min. Allow to cool. Make the almond paste. When cake has cooled, brush it with the glaze. Make the almond paste into 8 cones, and stand these at equal intervals round the top edge of the ring cake. Coat the cake and the cones with the icing. When it is nearly set, decorate the cake with 'jewels' made from glacé cherries, etc.

MAYPOLE CHILDREN'S PARTY CAKE

Recipe for Basic Butter Sponge Cake Green glacé icing	Gaily coloured pencil Narrow ribbon Small toys

Bake the Butter Sponge Cake in an 8-in sandwich-tin. When cold, ice the top with green icing. Insert the pencil upright in the centre. Attach lengths of ribbon to the top which will reach the edge of the cake. Fasten them to the edge of the cake, at equal intervals all round it; or attach the ribbon ends to the toys and place these round the cake.

DRUM CHILDREN'S PARTY CAKE

Recipe for 2 Basic Victoria Sandwich Cakes Apricot glaze or apricot marmalade	Recipe for 2 batches butter icing Brown food colouring or a little chocolate icing Small round yellow sweets (optional)
Recipe for 2 batches glacé icing 2 2-in bands shiny red paper to encircle cake	

Bake the Victoria Sandwich Cakes. When cold, cut each in half horizontally. Spread the cut surfaces with apricot glaze or marmalade, and sandwich together again with butter icing. Cut off the top of 1 cake so that it is level. Brush with apricot glaze or marmalade, and cover with a smooth layer of butter icing. Place the second cake on top, to make a 'drum' shape. Trim any projecting edges.
Cover the cake with smooth white glacé icing. Reserve a little icing, and tint it dark brown (or use chocolate icing if you prefer). Pipe diagonal lines from top to bottom of the cake, at intervals all round. When set, pipe similar lines slanting the opposite way, to make 'diamond' outlines. Pin one band of paper round the base of the cake. Pin the other round the top, so that it stands a little higher than the cake's surface. Decorate, if desired, with small yellow sweets to represent brass studs.

FAIRY COTTAGE CHILDREN'S PARTY CAKE

Recipe for rich dark gingerbread	Liquorice allsorts and other assorted small sweets
Apricot glaze	
Recipe for 2 batches glacé icing	
Brown and green food colouring	

Bake the gingerbread in 2 loaf-tins the same size. Turn out, and allow to cool. When cold, trim 1 loaf into a near brick-like block. Cut through the length of the second cake, from top to bottom, diagonally, forming 2 triangular 'sticks' for the roof. Brush both cakes with apricot glaze. Place the 2 triangular pieces 'back to back' on the block, making a roof.

Ice the walls of the 'cottage' with white icing. Tint some icing brown, and ice the roof. As the icing begins to set, decorate the cake with sweets for windows, door, chimney-pots, etc. Tint a little icing green, and spread it on the board or plate round the 'cottage' to represent grass.

HALLOWE'EN PARTY CAKE

Recipe for Basic Victoria Sandwich Cake	Chocolate finger biscuits
Recipe for 2 batches chocolate butter icing	A little glacé icing tinted red
Cocoa	Red foil paper
	Cotton wool

Make the Victoria Sandwich in a 2-pt pudding basin. Cool on a wire rack. When cold, ice with the chocolate butter icing, and scatter a little sieved cocoa over it. Dust the finger biscuits with cocoa, and pile them up round the cake, to make it look like a bonfire. Drip on red glacé icing to represent small flames, and add cotton wool for 'smoke'.

YULE LOG CHRISTMAS CAKE

Recipe for Chocolate Swiss Roll	White glacé icing
Recipe for chocolate butter icing	Almond paste tinted green or angelica
Cocoa	Small round red sweets

Make the Chocolate Swiss Roll as described, but fill with chocolate butter icing instead of vanilla. Dust the outside of the 'log' with cocoa, and decorate with lines of white glacé icing, to represent snow. Cut holly leaves from tinted almond paste or angelica, add sweets for berries, and use to decorate the cake.

If you wish, make 2 small extra Chocolate Swiss Rolls, and use them as side 'branches' for the 'log'.

EASTER EGG CAKE

Recipe for 2 Basic Victoria Sandwich Cakes	*or* **recipe for 2 batches coffee glacé icing**
Apricot glaze *or* **apricot marmalade**	**Small quantity brown food colouring (if glacé icing is used)** *or*
Recipe for almond paste, using 8 oz ground almonds	**chocolate icing Small yellow chicks and 1 larger chick**

Bake the Victoria Sandwich Cakes in 2 2-pt pudding basins. Turn out and cool on wire racks. When cold, stand 1 cake upright on its smaller end. Cut off the top if necessary so that it is level. Brush the cake all over with apricot glaze or marmalade. Cover the sides with a smooth layer of almond paste or coffee glacé icing. Cut the larger flat surface of the second cake so that it stands level. Brush with apricot glaze or marmalade. Invert the cake on to the first cake, to make an egg shape. Brush the top and sides of the second cake with apricot glaze or marmalade.

Carefully cut a small slice from the narrow top of the cake on top, leaving it attached at one side. Scoop out a very small amount of cake from underneath the cut slice. Brush the cut surfaces with apricot glaze or marmalade. Then cover this top cake with almond paste or glacé icing like the bottom one, including both sides of the cut slice and the inside of the scooped-out portion. Prop up the cut slice with a pencil while the icing sets. When it is set, pipe a line of dark-tinted glacé icing or chocolate icing round the edge of the cut slice, and place the largest chick inside the scooped-out 'shell', propping up the cut slice. Stand the smaller chicks round the base of the cake.

MOTHER'S CAKE
To be served on Mothering Sunday

Mixture: as for Birthday Cake baked in a 6-in tin.
Almond paste, using 6 oz ground almonds, etc
Royal icing, using 12 oz icing sugar, etc

Cover cake with almond paste and allow to dry. Pour over royal icing of coating consistency—make as smooth as possible and remove blisters by means of a hatpin or skewer; allow to firm before decorating. Place the cake on a cake board 1 in larger than the cake. Pipe a circle round the top rim of the cake with a ¼-in plain pipe. Leave to set, then pipe a second circle on top of the first, repeat a third time (but use a small plain pipe) and a fourth, if fancied. Pipe in the same way on the base. Make some yellow or red roses and some green leaves from coloured almond paste and use to decorate the top. Pipe on the words 'Mother's Day'.

SIMNEL CAKE

Mixture: as for Birthday Cake or any other fruit cake
Almond paste: 6 oz almonds, etc
Glacé icing: 2 oz icing sugar, etc

Line a 6- or 7-in cake-tin thickly. Cut off about ⅓ of the almond paste and roll out into a round slightly less than the diameter of the tin to be used. Place ½ the cake mixture in the tin, cover with a round of almond paste and place the remaining cake mixture on top. Bake in a moderate oven (180 °C, 350 °F, Gas 4) for ½ hr, reduce heat to cool (150–140 °C, 300–275 °F, Gas 2–1) for 2–2½ hr. Leave for 24 hr. Using about ½ the remaining almond paste, cover the top of the cake. With the remainder, make small balls and place these at even intervals round top edge of the cake. Brush them over with egg wash. Tie a band of greaseproof paper tightly round the top of the ake. Place in a hot oven until the balls are icely browned. When cool, pour glacé :ing into the centre of the cake and decor-te as required with almond-paste eggs, mall chicks, etc.

'his cake used to be served on Mother's)ay but is now usually served on Easter unday.

Cooking time—about 3 hr

'WELFTH NIGHT CAKE

oz butter *or* margarine	4 oz currants
	4 oz sultanas
oz brown sugar	4 oz mixed peel
eggs	½ level teasp
gill milk	ground cinnamon
level teasp	½ level teasp
icarbonate of	mixed spice
oda	¾ lb plain flour
oz treacle	¼ teasp salt

ine a 7-in cake-tin with greaseproof paper. Iream the fat and sugar and beat in the ggs gradually. Add the milk in which the oda is dissolved; stir in the treacle and eat well. Add the prepared fruit and oices. Sift in the flour and salt and mix ghtly. Put into the tin and bake in a arm oven (175 °C, 335 °F, Gas 3). Silver harms should be baked in the cake; wrap greaseproof paper.

Cooking time—2–2½ hr

'ALENTINE'S CAKE

oz butter *or* margarine	2 eggs
oz castor sugar	4 oz self-raising flour
rated rind of emon *or* orange	Pinch of salt

ECORATION

lacé icing using 2 oz icing ugar, etc	Red almond paste
	Green *or* chocolate almond paste

rease and dust with flour a heart-shaped n 7 in wide, shaking out any surplus flour. ream fat and sugar till white, and beat in the lemon or orange rind. Add the eggs one t a time and beat each until the mixture

is very light. Sift the flour and salt and fold into the mixture. Put the mixture into the tin. Bake in a moderate oven (180 °C, 350 °F, Gas 4) for ¾–1 hr. Allow to cool for a few minutes, then turn out.

When cold, coat the cake with the glacé icing and when the icing is firm enough— not too dry—decorate with two heart shapes cut out of red almond paste. Make an arrow of chocolate *or* green almond paste and place it to look as if it goes through the hearts.

RICH DARK GINGERBREAD

8 oz plain flour	2–4 oz crystallised ginger
⅛ teasp salt	
1–2 level teasp ground cinnamon	2 oz blanched and chopped almonds
1–2 level teasp mixed spice	4 oz butter *or* margarine
2 level teasp ground ginger	4 oz sugar
	4 oz treacle
2 oz dates *or* raisins *or* sultanas	2 eggs
	A little warm milk, if required
1 level teasp bicarbonate of soda	

Grease a 7-in tin and line the bottom with greaseproof paper, well greased, or silicone-treated paper.

Mix flour and salt and other dry ingredients with the prepared fruit, crystallised ginger cut into pieces, and almonds chopped roughly. Melt the fat, sugar and treacle, add to the dry ingredients with the beaten eggs. If the mixture seems stiff, add a little warm milk but do not make it too soft. Pour into the tin, and bake in a warm to cool oven (170–150 °C, 335–310 °F, Gas 3–2).

Cooking time—1¾ hr–2 hr

HOT CROSS BUNS

1 lb plain flour	½ oz yeast
½ teasp salt	1–2 eggs
2 oz margarine *or* margarine and lard	1½–2 gills milk
	2 oz currants *or*
	or 2 oz raisins
4 oz sugar	and peel
1 teasp mixed spice *or* cinnamon	Short crust pastry trimmings

Mix salt with warmed flour. Rub in fat. Add sugar, spice, creamed yeast, and eggs with the warm milk. Mix to a soft, light dough, beat well and put to rise. When well risen, knead the dough lightly, working in the fruit, and divide into 20–24 pieces. Form into round shapes, flatten slightly and put to prove for 15 min. Cut narrow strips of pastry 1½–2 in long, brush tops of buns with egg wash *or* milk, place pastry crosses on top and bake in a hot oven (220 °C, 425 °F, Gas 7).

20–24 buns   *Cooking time—15–20 min*

BLACK BUN FOR A SCOTS' NEW YEAR'S EVE

PASTRY

1 lb plain flour	5 oz butter *or*
¼ teasp salt	margarine
¾ level teasp	Water to mix
baking-powder	

FILLING

2 lb currants	1 teasp ground
1½ lb valencia	ginger
raisins	1 teasp allspice
2 oz glacé	1 teasp black
cherries	pepper
½ lb sultanas	2 level teasp
2 oz chopped peel	bicarbonate of
6 oz blanched,	soda
chopped almonds	2 level teasp
½ lb sugar	cream of tartar
¾ lb plain flour	1 egg
2 level teasp	Milk to bind
ground cinnamon	

Make the pastry: sift flour, salt and baking-powder, rub in the margarine and mix with water to a stiff dough.
Mix prepared fruit and nuts with flour, sugar, spices and raising agents for the filling, add the egg and milk to mix stiffly.
Line a greased 7-in or 8-in cake-tin with ⅔ of the pastry, put in the mixture and make level, wet the edges. Roll out the remaining ⅓ of pastry, place on top and neaten the edges. Prick well all over the top, brush with egg and bake in a very cool oven (150 °C, 300 °F, Gas 1–2).

Cooking time—4–5 hr

FESTIVE GATEAU

2 oz plain flour	1 oz grated
4 large eggs	Bournville choco
1 oz ground	late
hazelnuts	1 oz butter,
	melted

FILLING AND DECORATION

2 oz Bournville	1 level tablesp
chocolate	sifted icing suga
¼ pt double cream	

Grease and line two 7-in sandwich tins twice. Whisk the eggs and sugar together. Gently stir in the chocolate and flour. Fol in the melted butter; divide the mixtur evenly between the tins and bake in moderate oven, 180 °C, 350 °F, Gas Mar 4, for 20 minutes.
To complete the cake, roast the hazelnut in a hot oven for 2–3 minutes, then remov skins by rubbing in a cloth. Break th chocolate and put into a basin standin over a pan of hot water until melted. Leav to cool. Whip the cream; fold in the icin sugar alternately with the cooled chocola and sandwich the cakes together with ha the chocolate cream, then spread th remainder over the top. Mark with a forl

ICEBOX CAKE

6 oz icing sugar	2 tablesp lemon
4 oz butter	juice
2 medium eggs	48 sponge finger
2 teasp grated	biscuits
lemon peel	

Cream butter and sugar until light an fluffy, and work in eggs one at a time Gradually add lemon peel and juice an beat hard until fluffy and smooth. Cover piece of cardboard with foil and on it plac 12 biscuits, curved side down. Spread o one-third of creamed mixture. Put anothe layer of biscuits in opposite direction, an more creamed mixture. Repeat layers an end with a layer of biscuits. Wrap in foi and chill in the refrigerator for sever; hours. To serve, leave at room temperatu for 1 hr. Then unwrap, and cover wit whipped cream.

Children's Parties

SMALL CHILDREN love a party, especially a birthday party. Colourful small cakes and other food appeal to them, although they like it to be familiar, something they know. They like savouries too, more than we sometimes realise. All food for small children should be in small portions, and easy to eat without making a mess.

SAUSAGE SNACKS

Cooked whole or halved, small sausages make attractive snacks when brightly garnished. Halve sausages crosswise and set each, cut side down, on a small toasted croûte. Spear whole sausages on wooden cocktail picks, and stick these into a large grapefruit or small melon with a thin slice cut from the bottom so that it stands level. Top sausages with maraschino cherries, pickled onions, cheese cubes and chunks of canned pineapple.

Frankfurter sausages can be treated in the same way, or can be split lengthwise and filled with cream cheese before being speared on cocktail sticks.

POTATO CRISPS

6 egg-sized, waxy potatoes	Deep fat Salt

Scrub and rinse the potatoes. Slice very thinly with a sharp knife or on a potato slicer bought for the purpose. Drop them into cold water as they are cut. Drain and rinse and dry well between the folds of a clean cloth. Sprinkle gradually into hot deep fat, at 320 °F, and fry till golden and crisp. Remove from the fat as they brown and drain on absorbent paper. Keep them hot while frying the rest. Sprinkle with salt. They can be kept in an air-tight tin for some time and be re-heated when necessary.

Note: To the professional cook or chef these are known as 'chips'. They are served with grills and with poultry and game but may also be served with many meat and fish dishes.

6 helpings　　　　　*Cooking time—3–4 min*

SAUSAGE ROLLS

Rough puff pastry using 4 oz flour, etc	½ lb sausages Egg yolk to glaze

Roll out the pastry and cut into 8 even-sized squares. Skin the sausages. Divide the sausage meat into 8 portions and make each piece into a roll the same length as the pastry. Place the sausage meat on the pastry, wet the edge and fold over leaving

Sausage rolls

Sausage snacks

the ends open. Knock up the edges with the back of a knife. Make three incisions on top. Brush over with beaten egg and place on a baking-sheet. Bake in a hot oven (220°C, 425°F, Gas 7) until the pastry is well risen and brown. Reduce the heat and continue baking till the pastry is cooked.

Note: Small sausage rolls can be quickly made by rolling the pastry into an oblong. Form the sausage meat into long rolls the length of the pastry, place the meat on the pastry then divide the pastry into strips wide enough to encircle the meat. Damp one edge of each strip, fold over and press together firmly. Cut into rolls of the desired length, finish as above.

Home-made sausage 'spiral' rolls are a decorative alternative. Use whole small sausages with skins. Roll out the pastry into a long strip about ½ in wide. Wrap pastry strip diagonally round each sausage, leaving a small gap between strip edges. Bake as above.

8 sausage rolls   *Cooking time—about ½ hr*

SMALL PLAIN CAKES

For small plain cakes, use the variations suggested under Basic Plain Buns. Small 'butter sponge' cakes can be cut from a Basic Butter Sponge or Victoria Sandwich cake baked in a square or oblong tin. For small sponge cakes and rich cakes use the mixture below. The Butterfly Orange Cakes are particularly attractive for a children's party.

BASIC SMALL SPONGE CAKES

3 oz plain flour	1 level teasp
Pinch of salt	baking-powder
3 eggs	½ teasp vanilla
3 oz sugar	essence

Make like the Basic Large Sponge Cake. Put the mixture into oblong sponge cake-tins prepared by greasing and dusting with equal quantities of flour and castor sugar. Half-fill the tins and dredge the tops with castor sugar. Bake in a moderate oven

Small butterflies

180–170 °C, 350–325 °F, Gas 4–3) until well risen, firm and a pale fawn colour.

0–12 cakes   *Cooking time—20 min*

BASIC SMALL 'RICH' CAKES

The following is a suitable mixture for all these small cakes and can be varied in many ways.

BASIC RECIPE

2 oz butter *or* **margarine**	**Pinch of salt**
2 oz castor sugar	**Water** *or* **milk** **as required**
1 egg	
3 oz self-raising flour *or* **3 oz plain flour and 1 level teasp baking-powder**	

Beat the fat and sugar until creamy and white. Whisk the egg and add gradually; beat well between each addition. Sift together the flour, salt and baking-powder. Gently stir the flour, etc, into the creamed fat; add milk or water to make a soft dropping consistency. Half-fill greased bun-tins with the mixture and bake in a fairly hot to moderate oven (190–180 °C, 375–350 °F, Gas 5–4).

Note: This mixture can be baked in paper cases and decorated with glacé icing or cherries.

10–12 cakes   *Cooking time—15–20 min*

VARIATIONS OF BASIC RECIPE

Cherry Cakes
Add 1–2 oz coarsely chopped glacé cherries with the flour.

Chocolate Cakes
Sift ½ oz cocoa with the flour, and add a few drops of vanilla essence with the water or milk. The cakes can be iced with chocolate glacé icing.

Coconut Cakes
Add ½ oz coconut with the flour and add ¼ teasp vanilla essence with the milk or water.

Lemon or Orange Cakes
Add the grated rind of 1 lemon or orange with the flour, and ice with lemon or orange glacé icing.

Madeleines
Bake the basic mixture in greased dariole or castle pudding moulds. Turn out when baked; cool. Spread all round, top and side, with warmed apricot jam. Roll in desiccated coconut and decorate with ½ glacé cherry.

Nut Cakes
Add 1–2 oz coarsely chopped walnuts, almonds or hazelnuts, with the flour.

Queen Cakes
Add 1–2 oz currants *or* sultanas with the flour, or a few currants may be placed in the bottom of each queen cake-tin and the mixture placed on top.

BUTTERFLY ORANGE CAKES

The basic mixture for small rich cakes, flavoured with orange, and cooked in greased bouchée-tins
1 gill sweetened cream, flavoured with orange liqueur *or* essence
A little apricot jam

Cut a thin slice from the top of each cake. Cut each slice in two, to make two wings. Dredge with icing sugar. Spread the cut top of each cake with a little jam, pipe a rosette of whipped cream on this, and place the wings in position.

10–12 cakes

BASIC BISCUIT RECIPE
(Shrewsbury Biscuits)

4 oz butter *or* **margarine**	**½ level teasp ground cinnamon**
4 oz castor sugar	*or* **1 teasp grated**
1 small egg	**lemon rind**
8 oz plain flour	**Milk as required**

Cream the fat and sugar and beat in the egg. Sift flour with cinnamon, *or* add grated rind, and add to the creamed fat mixture. Mix to a stiff consistency, using milk if required. Roll out fairly thinly and cut out with a 2½-in cutter. Place on a greased baking-sheet and bake in a moderate oven (180 °C, 350 °F, Gas 4) till light fawn colour.

30–32 biscuits   *Cooking time—15–20 min*

EASTERTIDE BISCUITS

Add ½ level teasp mixed spice and 2 oz currants to the basic recipe for Shrewsbury Biscuits. Roll out mixture to ¼-in thickness and cut into 4-in rounds. If desired, brush with egg white and dredge with sugar. Bake in a moderate oven (180 °C, 350 °F, Gas 4) until golden-brown.

12–16 biscuits   *Cooking time—20–30 min*

ANIMAL BISCUITS

Use the Basic Biscuit Recipe, cut out with an animal-shaped cutter; decorate with faces in chocolate or coffee glacé icing.

MELTING MOMENTS

2 oz lard *or* hydrogenated shortening	½ egg
	½ teasp vanilla essence
2 oz margarine	5 oz self-raising flour
3 oz sugar	Cornflakes

Cream fat and sugar and beat in egg. Add flavouring, stir in the sifted flour and with wet hands make into balls the size of marbles and roll in crushed cornflakes. Bake in a fairly hot to moderate oven (190–180 °C, 375–350 °F, Gas 5–4).

24 biscuits   *Cooking time—15 min*

GINGER SNAPS

6 oz self-raising flour	3–4 oz. sugar
Pinch of salt	2 oz lard *or* shortening
1 level teasp bicarbonate of soda	1½ oz golden syrup
2 level teasp ground ginger	1 egg

Note: Take small measure of bicarbonate and ginger.
Sift flour, salt, soda and ginger; add sugar. Melt lard and syrup, cool slightly, then add to dry ingredients; add the egg. Divide into 24 pieces and make into balls, place well apart on greased baking-sheets. Bake in a fairly hot to moderate oven (190–180 °C, 375–350 °F, Gas 5–4) till a good rich brown colour.

24 Ginger Snaps   *Cooking time—20 min*

COCONUT PYRAMIDS

3 egg whites	8 oz desiccated coconut
1½ oz rice flour	
4–5 oz castor sugar	½ teasp vanilla essence
	Rice paper

Whisk the egg whites very stiffly, stir in lightly the rice flour, castor sugar, coconut and essence. Put the mixture in small close heaps on rice paper; bake in a cool oven (150 °C, 300 °F, Gas 2) till they are light brown.

18 pyramids

BIRTHDAY CAKE
(1 FRUIT and 2 BUTTER SPONGE)

Ingredients for (1)

4 oz butter *or* margarine	1 level teasp mixed spice
4 oz soft brown sugar	11 oz mixed fruit—sultanas, currants, glacé cherries
1½ oz golden syrup	
2 eggs	
6 oz plain flour	2 oz candied peel *or* marmalade
⅛ teasp salt	
1 level teasp baking-powder	½ gill milk (approx)

For the older child, a birthday cake should be a fruit cake.
Line a 6–7-in cake-tin. Cream fat, sugar and syrup thoroughly. Whisk eggs and add alternately with the sifted flour, salt and baking-powder, beating well with each addition. Add remaining ingredients and fruit, which has been mixed with a little of the flour. Mix to a fairly soft consistency with milk and place in the cake-tin. Bake for ½ hr in a moderate oven (180 °C, 390 °F, Gas 4) and a further 2–2½ hr in a cool oven (150–140 °C, 300–275 °F, Gas 2–1).

For a younger child, a 'butter sponge' birthday cake is more suitable than a fruit cake. A most attractive cake can be made from enough of the basic Butter Sponge Cake mixture to fill 3 7-in sandwich-tins. One third of the mixture should be coloured with a few drops of food colouring before being put in its tin; and, after baking, it should be 'sandwiched' between the other two layers, to make a coloured layer between them.
A fruit cake is usually coated with almond paste and decorated with royal icing. But a sponge cake can be decorated most successfully with a butter icing, or American frosting.

Cooking time—about 3 hr (fruit cake)
40 min (butter sponge)

Birthday cake

BASIC BUTTER SPONGE CAKE

4 oz butter *or* margarine	6 oz self-raising flour
6 oz castor sugar	Pinch salt
4 eggs	1 level teasp baking-powder
	2 dessertsp cold water to mix

Make like a Victoria Sandwich Cake.

AMERICAN FROSTING

8 oz granulated sugar	1 egg white, beaten
4 tablesp water	with flavouring

Put the sugar and water into a pan. Dissolve the sugar slowly in the water, then bring to boiling point. Boil to 130 °C, 240 °F without stirring. Brush down the sides of the pan with a brush dipped in cold water, and remove scum as it rises.

Pour on to the beaten egg white and flavouring, beating all the time. Continue beating until the icing begins to thicken and coats the back of a spoon thickly. Pour quickly over the cake. Spread with a palette knife, and work up the icing in swirls. You can also use the icing as a filling. ½ teasp vanilla essence or lemon juice and a pinch of cream of tartar are the most usual additions. For other flavourings, see Butter Icings.

FUDGE

1 lb granulated sugar	2 oz butter
¼ pt milk	½ teasp vanilla essence

Put sugar and milk in a saucepan and leave to soak for 1 hr. Add the butter, place over gentle heat and stir until sugar is dissolved. Then bring to boil and boil to the 'small ball' degree (237 °F). Remove from heat, stir in vanilla, cool slightly, then beat until thick. Pour into an oiled tin; cut in squares when cold.
Note: Coconut, nuts or ginger may be stirred in while fudge is cooling. **Chocolate fudge:** Add 2 tablesp cocoa or 2 oz plain chocolate with the butter.

BUTTER ICING OR BUTTER CREAM FILLING (1) (quick)

2 oz butter *or* margarine	Flavouring
3 oz icing sugar	Pinch of salt
	Colouring

Cream the butter or margarine. Add the sugar and salt gradually and cream together. Beat until smooth, creamy and pale. Add flavouring and colouring to taste.

FLAVOURINGS

Almond Beat in ¼ teasp almond essence.

Chocolate Dissolve 1 oz chocolate in 1 tablesp water and beat in, *or* beat in 1 dessertsp cocoa and a few drops of vanilla essence.

Coffee Beat in 1 dessertsp coffee essence.

Jam Add 1 tablesp strong-flavoured jam, e.g. plum, raspberry.

Birthday cake with butter icing

Lemon Beat in 1 teasp strained lemon juice.

Orange Beat in 1 dessertsp strained orange juice.

Vanilla Beat in ½ teasp vanilla essence.

Walnut Add 2 oz chopped walnuts and 1–2 teasp coffee essence.

In cold weather, you may warm the butter slightly, but do not let it oil. This butter icing always has a slight taste of raw sugar. A better but more costly one is made thus:

BUTTER ICING OR BUTTER CREAM (2)

4–6 oz castor sugar	4 oz unsalted butter (for filling) *or* 8 oz unsalted butter (for icing) **Flavouring as above**
4 egg yolks	
¼ pt milk	

Beat the egg yolks until fluffy, and then beat in the sugar gradually until the mixture is thick and very pale. Heat the milk and when at boiling point, trickle it into the egg yolk mixture beating all the time. Return the mixture to the milk saucepan and heat it gently until it thickens. Place the saucepan in a pan of cold water to cool, cover, and beat often enough to prevent a skin forming. When the custard is tepid beat in the flavouring and butter alternately. Chill if required very stiff.

MARSHMALLOWS

¼ lb gum arabic	3 egg whites
½ pt water	Caramel essence
½ lb icing sugar	

Soak the gum arabic in the water until soft, then heat gently until dissolved, and strain it through fine muslin. Return to the pan, add the sugar, and when dissolved, stir in the egg whites, and whisk until the mixture is quite stiff. Flavour to taste, and let it remain for about 10 hr. When ready, cut into small squares, and dredge them thickly with icing sugar.

NOUGAT

8 oz almonds	4 oz honey
4 oz icing sugar	2 egg whites

Blanch and dry the almonds thoroughly. Line a box of suitable size first with white paper and then with wafer paper, both of which must be cut to fit exactly. Put the sugar, honey and egg whites into a sugar boiler or pan, and stir over a low heat until the mixture becomes thick and white. Drop a little into cold water; if it hardens immediately, remove the pan from the heat, and stir in the almonds. Dredge the slab with icing sugar, turn on to it the nougat, and form into a ball. Press into the prepared box, cover with paper, let it remain under pressure until cold, then cut up into squares.

Teen-agers' Parties

DEVILS ON HORSEBACK

1–2 chickens' livers or 3–4 oz calf's liver	8 well-drained prunes, cooked
Butter	8 short thin rindless rashers streaky bacon
Salt and pepper	
Cayenne pepper	4 small bread squares
	Olives stuffed with pimento

Gently cook the liver in a little butter, then cut it into 8 pieces. Season well and dust with a few grains of cayenne pepper. Stone the prunes and stuff with the liver. Stretch the bacon to double its size with the flat of a knife. Encircle each prune in a piece of bacon, secure with a wooden cocktail stick and bake in a very hot oven. Fry the bread in shallow bacon fat and drain well. Remove sticks and place the 'devils' on the bread. Garnish each with a pimento-stuffed olive.

KEDGEREE

1 lb cold cooked fish (smoked haddock is generally preferred)	2 hard-boiled eggs
	2 oz butter
	Salt and pepper
¼ lb rice	Cayenne pepper

Boil and dry the rice. Divide the fish into small flakes. Cut the whites of the eggs into slices and sieve the yolks. Melt the butter in a saucepan, add to it the fish, rice, egg whites, salt, pepper and cayenne and stir until hot. Turn the mixture on to a hot dish. Press into the shape of a pyramid with a fork, decorate with egg yolk and serve as hot as possible.

5–6 helpings   *Cooking time—40–50 min*

BACON OLIVES

3 oz finely-chopped cooked or canned meat	½ teasp finely-chopped parsley
1 oz finely-chopped cooked ham or tongue	¼ teasp powdered mixed herbs
	Nutmeg
1½ tablesp bread-crumbs	Salt and pepper
	1 egg
½ teasp finely-chopped onion	8 small thin rashers of bacon

Mix the meat, ham, breadcrumbs, onion, parsley and herbs together, add a pinch of nutmeg, season to taste with salt and pepper. Stir in gradually as much egg as is necessary to bind the mixture together. Leave for ½ hr, then divide into 8 portions. Form each portion into a cork shape, roll in a rasher of bacon, and secure with string

Seafood flan

Brandy snaps

Apple loaf

Stuffed ham rolls

or small skewers. Bake in a fairly hot oven (190 °C, 375 °F, Gas 5) for about ½ hr. Serve on toast.

SEA FOOD FLAN

2 oz butter *or* margarine	4 oz crushed plain biscuits
¼ teasp salt	(cream crackers)
1 oz soft cheese	

FILLING

1 dessertsp gelatine	1 teasp finely-chopped onion
½ 3-oz can pink salmon *or* tuna	1 teasp finely-chopped parsley
6 sardines	Salt and pepper
1 gill mayonnaise	to taste
2 tablesp tomato ketchup	

To make the flan case. Cream fat, salt and cheese together and knead in the crushed biscuits. Place mixture on a plate and mould it into a greased 7-in flan ring. Put into refrigerator until firmly set. Remove flan ring.

Dissolve gelatine in 3 tablesp hot water. Flake the salmon or tuna and sardines (free from bones) and mix together all ingredients for filling. When beginning to set, pour into prepared flan case. Decorate with hard-boiled egg and shelled prawns.

BAKED AND STUFFED POTATOES

6 large potatoes

STUFFING, choice of

1) **3 oz grated cheese; 1 oz butter *or* margarine; a little milk; seasoning; nutmeg**
2) **3 oz chopped, fried bacon; a little milk; seasoning**
3) **3 oz mashed, cooked smoked haddock; chopped parsley; lemon juice; a little milk; nutmeg**
4) **2 boned kippers, cooked and mashed; little milk**
5) **2 oz grated cheese; 1 oz butter; chopped parsley; a little milk; seasoning; 2 egg yolks stirred into the filling; 2 egg whites folded in at the end**
6) **3 oz minced steak; ½ small minced onion and seasoning; sautéed and mixed**

Scrub, rinse and dry the potatoes and grease them. With a small sharp knife, cut through the skin of the potatoes to give the appearance of a lid. Bake for 1–1½ hr at 190 °C, 375 °F, Gas 5. Lift off lids carefully, scoop out cooked potato from skins, including lids, taking care not to split the skins. Mash the potato in a basin and add the ingredients of any one of the stuffings listed above. Mix well and season thoroughly. Fill the potato skins with the mixture, piling it high. Fork the tops and brush with a little egg, or sprinkle with a little grated cheese (if an ingredient of the stuffing). Put back in the oven and bake till thoroughly hot and golden-brown. Serve in a hot dish garnished with parsley and with the skin 'lids' replaced, if liked.

Note: A stuffing consisting of cooked minced meat in a sauce or gravy *or* of cooked mixed vegetables *or* flaked fish in a sauce may replace the floury meal of the potato entirely. The latter should then be mashed and served separately *or* mashed and piped round the opening of the potato after it has been stuffed and before returning it to the oven.

6 helpings   *Cooking time—about 2 h*

HAMBURGERS

1 lb minced beef	Salt and pepper
½ cup dry bread-crumbs	1 small onion, minced
½ cup milk	

Mix together all the ingredients. Form mixture into 6 patties, brown quickly on both sides in hot fat, reduce heat and cook more slowly until done, turning occasionally. Serve in round, split toasted rolls.

HAM ROLLS

4 thin slices of cooked ham	1–2 tablesp sweet chutney
2 oz cream cheese	Crisp lettuce

Spread each slice of ham on a board, trim

off surplus fat. Mix the cream cheese and chutney together, spread over the ham and roll. Put on to lettuce leaves. If wished cut the slices into 1-in lengths and instead of putting on to lettuce leaves put on small buttered biscuits and garnish with watercress leaves.

4 helpings or *12 small savouries*

PARTY SKEWERS

Make a mixed grill with sausage, kidney, liver, mushroom, bacon rolls, small onion rings and small squares of fried bread. Cut the pieces of food into small 1-in pieces when cooked, leaving the bacon rolls whole. Have ready some clean wooden orange sticks and arrange 4 or 5 pieces of food on each stick. Keep the food hot until served.

CHICKEN VOL-AU-VENT

6 oz cooked chicken	1 oz cooked noodles
Puff pastry, frozen *or* using	2–4 mushrooms
8 oz flour, etc	Salt, pepper, nutmeg
2 oz cooked ham *or* tongue	$\frac{1}{2}$ pt Béchamel sauce
	Egg *or* milk to glaze

Prepare the pastry; roll out to $\frac{3}{4}$ in thickness. Cut into a round or oval shape and place on a wet baking-sheet. Cut an inner ring through half the depth of the pastry and brush top of pastry (not sides) with beaten egg. Bake in a hot oven (220–230 °C, 425–450 °F, Gas 7) until well risen, firm and brown (about 25 min). Dice chicken and ham, slice mushrooms; add all these with the noodles to the Béchamel sauce, season well and heat thoroughly. Lift centre from vol-au-vent case and reserve for lid, clear any soft paste which may be inside, fill with the mixture, and replace lid.
A separate piece of pastry the size of the lid may be baked with the large case, and used as a lid for the filled case; this has a better appearance.
Alternatively make the pastry into six individual cases, and use the following filling:

FILLING

One 10$\frac{1}{2}$ oz can condensed Cream of Mushroom soup	2 oz cooked ham, diced
8 oz cooked chicken *or* turkey meat, diced	1–2 tablesp cream (optional)

Heat the chicken and ham gently in the soup, then add the cream if used. Fill the prepared cases. Put them into a preheated moderate oven (180 °C, 350 °F, Gas 4) to warm through and crisp. Serve hot or cold, with a crisp salad.

6 helpings

SAUSAGES (COCKTAIL, FRANKFURTER AND LARGE)

Cocktail sausages are best baked. Separate the sausages, prick them with a fork and lay in a baking-tin. Bake without extra fat at 180 °C, 350 °F, Gas 4 for about 10 min until brown on top. Turn, and bake a further 7–10 min to brown the underneath.
Frankfurters are treated like large sausages (*see* below). Alternatively, they can be pricked and simmered in white wine with a pinch of thyme until tender (about 10 min).
Large sausages Prick large sausages first with a fork, throw into boiling water and simmer for 15 min. Put into a frying-pan containing a little hot fat, and fry gently, turning to brown on all sides. To fry large sausages heat slowly to prevent the sausages bursting.

SAUSAGE AND APPLE MASH

$\frac{1}{2}$ lb sausages	Pinch of curry powder
3 tomatoes, halved	1 teasp lemon juice
1 lb potatoes	
1 oz butter	Salt and pepper
$\frac{1}{4}$ pt apple sauce	Chopped parsley

Fry the sausages gently until brown all over and cooked thoroughly. Add the tomatoes to the pan and cook gently. Meanwhile, boil the potatoes, drain and mash well. Add the

Macaroni au gratin with bacon rolls

Sausage and apple mash

butter, heated apple sauce, curry powder, lemon juice and seasoning and mix well. Spoon or pipe on to a warm serving dish, arrange the sausages and tomatoes on top and decorate with parsley.

Alternatively, leave out the tomatoes, and instead of adding apple sauce to the potato, use plain mashed potato and add grilled apple slices to the dish as a garnish.

2 helpings

MEAT BALLS

1 small onion	1 teasp potato
A little lard	flour
4 oz raw beef	1½ teasp salt
2½ oz pork	¼ teasp white
1–1½ cups milk	pepper
1 egg	1 teasp sugar
2 tablesp bread-	1–2 tablesp butter
crumbs	or cream
	(optional)

Peel, slice and fry onions slightly in a little lard. Wash meat and pass 3 times through mincer, together with the fried onion or blend in an electric blender for a few seconds. Mix milk and egg; soak bread-crumbs and flour in this, add salt, pepper, sugar, cream or butter (if used) and finally the meat. Mix well. Make into small balls and fry brown in butter or fat.

Meat balls are a favourite dish in Sweden and can be eaten fried or boiled with potato salad with various sauces; mush-room and tomato, etc.

4 helpings

CHEESE AND ONION PIE

Short crust	½ oz flour
pastry, frozen *or*	Salt and pepper
using 8 oz flour,	4 oz cheese
etc., if home-made	2 tablesp milk
3 small onions	

Parboil the onions whilst making the pastry.

Line an 8-in fireproof plate with half the pastry. Mix the salt and pepper with the flour. Slice the onions and dip in the seasoned flour, spread them over the

bottom of the lined plate. Grate the cheese and sprinkle it over the onion, add the milk. Wet the edge of the pastry, put on the cover and press the edges firmly together. Knock up the edges, decorate as desired and brush over with milk. Bake in a hot oven (220 °C, 425 °F, Gas 7) for about 40 min.

This can be made as an open tart if liked, using 4 oz flour, etc, for the pastry.

6–8 helpings

SCOTCH EGGS

3 hard-boiled eggs	Egg and bread-
½ lb sausage meat	crumbs
	Frying fat

Shell the eggs and cover each egg with sausage meat. If liked, a little finely chopped onion can be mixed with the sausage meat before using. Coat carefully with beaten egg and breadcrubs, fry in hot fat until nicely browned. Cut each egg in half. Scotch eggs can be served either hot or cold.

3 helpings

CHEESE FLAN

CHEESE PASTRY	FILLING
8 oz plain flour	1 egg
Pinch of salt and	¼ pt milk
cayenne pepper	3 oz grated
4 oz butter	Cheddar cheese
4 oz grated	Pinch of salt
Cheddar cheese	A few grains
1 egg yolk	cayenne pepper
Little cold water	
to mix	

Sieve flour and seasonings into a basin. Rub in the butter until mixture resembles fine breadcrumbs. Stir in cheese, and bind together with egg yolk and water. Roll out on a floured board to ¼-in thick and line a greased sandwich tin, approx 8 in long and 1 in deep. Bake 'blind' filled with baking beans in a fairly hot oven (200 °C, 400 °F, Gas 6) for 20 min. Remove beans and greaseproof paper and return to oven for further 5 min. Cool, and remove flan from tin.

To make the filling, beat the egg, mil most of the grated cheese and the seasonin together. Pour into the flan case, sprink with the remaining cheese, and bake in fairly hot oven (200 °C, 400 °F, Gas 6) f about 20 min until the top is golden-brow Serve hot.

4 helpings

MACARONI AU GRATIN WITH BACON ROLLS

4 oz macaroni	Salt and pepper
1 pt white sauce	Browned bread-
4 oz grated cheese	crumbs *or* 1 oz
Bacon rashers	finely grated
	Cheddar cheese
	Butter

Break the macaroni into pieces about 1½ long, put them into rapidly boiling salte water and boil for about 20 min, or un the macaroni is tender. (If not required fi immediate use, cover the macaroni wi cold water to prevent the pieces stickir together.) Cover the bottom of a wel buttered baking-dish with white sauc sprinkle liberally with cheese, seasoning taste, and add a layer of macaroni. Repe the layers, cover the last layer of macaroni thickly with sauce, sprinkle the surfac lightly with breadcrumbs or extra grate cheese and add a few small pieces of butte Bake in a hot oven (220 °C, 425 °F, Gas for about 20 min.

Cut the rind off the rashers, roll each or up and place in a baking tin with the c ends underneath. Bake under the macaroi dish for 10–15 min until the bacon rolls ar crisp. Use as a garnish, or serve separatel

6–7 helpings

GRILLED LIVER 'BITES'

Use lambs' or chickens' livers. Cut int neat pieces about 1 in across, making sur that no tubes are left in them, and that the are free of fat and gristle. Mix salt an freshly ground black pepper in a plasti bag with enough flour to coat the live pieces. Add a pinch of paprika or cayenn pepper if you wish. Toss the liver pieces i the flour in the bag. Lift out, shake o excess flour. Heat the grill, and grill th pieces briefly, turning them once. A moment or two should be long enough, as they should still be slightly pink inside when done.

GRILLED BACON ROLLS

Cut the rind off thin rashers, roll each one up and fasten with a wooden cocktail stick. Heat the grill, and grill the rolls on all sides, turning them often. Remove the sticks (which will be charred) before serving.

ONION RINGS FOR A MIXED GRILL

Peel and slice small or medium-sized onions, and separate the rings. Dry well in a paper towel. Heat deep fat until hazing, and fry the onion rings until soft and turning brown. Drain over the pan on a perforated spoon, and then on kitchen paper.

FRIED BREAD FOR A MIXED GRILL

Small squares of bread without crusts can be deep-fried. They must be turned once in the hot fat, and drained as soon as they are slightly brown. They burn easily. Alternatively, they can be shallow-fried, like croûtes. Make sure that the first side is crisp before turning, as otherwise the bread will stay soggy.

MIXED GRILL

Use the recipes for baked cocktail sausages, grilled liver 'bites', grilled bacon rolls, onion rings and fried bread above. Add the recipes for grilled kidneys and grilled mushrooms from elsewhere in this book, and also the recipes for fried eggs and grilled lamb cutlets if you like.

Cook all your chosen ingredients, beginning with the ones which will take longest (usually cutlets). Fry eggs and grill liver 'bites' and mushrooms last. Keep hot until required. Sprinkle with chopped parsley and a few drops of melted butter

and lemon juice just before serving, if you are not serving a sauce.

APPLE LOAF

1 lb plain flour, sifted	**1 cooking apple, peeled, cored and sliced**
Pinch of salt	**Milk to mix**
1 teasp baking-powder	**4 oz icing sugar, sifted**
4 oz butter	**A little water**
4 oz lard	**1 tart eating apple (red), cored and sliced**
2 eggs, beaten	
2 oz currants	
2 oz raisins, seeded	

Dip the fruit in a little lemon juice as soon as prepared, to prevent discoloration.
Sift together the flour, salt and baking-powder. Rub in the fat, mix in the beaten egg, currants, raisins, cooking apple and milk. Mix well. Turn into a 1-lb lined loaf-tin, and bake in a moderate oven at 190 °C, 375 °F, Gas 5 for 40–45 min, or until springy and browned. When cool, spread the loaf with a thin icing made with icing sugar and water, and decorate with sliced eating apple. Serve for high tea, especially when salads are scarce.

6–8 helpings

TRIFLE (TRADITIONAL)

4 individual sponge cakes	**1 oz almonds (blanched and shredded)**
Raspberry *or* **strawberry jam**	**$\frac{1}{2}$ pt custard using $\frac{1}{2}$ pt milk, 1 egg and 1 egg yolk**
6 macaroons	
12 miniature macaroons	
$\frac{1}{4}$ pt sherry	**$\frac{1}{4}$ pt double cream**
Grated rind of $\frac{1}{2}$ lemon	**1 egg white**
	1–2 oz castor sugar

DECORATION

Glacé cherries	**Angelica**

Split the sponge cakes into two and spread the lower halves with jam. Replace tops. Arrange in a glass dish and cover with macaroons and miniatures. Soak with sherry, and sprinkle with lemon rind and almonds. Cover with the custard and leave to cool. Whisk the cream, egg white and sugar together until stiff and pile on top of the trifle. Decorate with glacé cherries and angelica.

Fruit trifles, such as Apricot or Gooseberry, are made by substituting layers of puréed or chopped fruit for the jam.

6 helpings

BRANDY SNAPS

2½ oz sugar	1 oz plain flour
1 oz butter *or* margarine	1 level teasp ground ginger
1 oz golden syrup	

Cream sugar, fat and syrup, and stir in the sifted flour and ginger. Make into 12–16 small balls and place well apart on greased baking-sheets—these biscuits spread. Bake in a cool oven (150 °C, 300 °F, Gas 2) until rich brown colour. Allow to cool slightly, remove from sheet with a knife and, while soft enough, roll round the handle of a wooden spoon, remove when set. The snaps may be filled with sweetened and flavoured cream.

12–16 Brandy snaps

Cooking time—10–15 mi

FRUIT PUNCH

2 lb large fleshy cooking apples	1 large can of pears (only a little fruit is required)
6 oz sugar	
2 pt water	
2 lemons	A few cherries
	1 qt ginger beer *or* cider

Peel and core the apples and cut up small. Simmer with the sugar, water and rind of the lemons for 15 min in a covered saucepan. Strain through muslin and allow the liquid to cool. Add to this the liquid from the pears and the juice of the lemons. Ston a few cherries, spear on cocktail sticks and put them in the glasses. Dice a little of the pears and put a few pieces in each glass together with some thinly peeled pieces of lemon rind if liked. Add the ginger beer or cider to the pear and apple juice mixture and serve in the glasses.

Informal Parties

An INFORMAL PARTY can be planned or 'just happen', and it may or may not have a theme. Food can be served on a buffet, or on small tables from which people help themselves. It may be any kind of fare, depending on the time of day or night, the weather and the party's theme, if it has one; but it usually consists of finger or fork food, or other easy-to-eat dishes.
Wine and cheese, beer and sausage, and pancake parties are all informal parties with a theme.
For a wine and cheese party, serve either a selection of cheeses from one country, or just one or two really big pieces of cheese; they look more dramatic than small wedges. Decorate cheeses with various fresh fruits in contrasting colours, and offer crisp lettuce leaves and scraped raw celery sticks in mugs instead of more formal salads. Serve home-made breads from other sections of this book with the cheeses, and follow with ice creams and really hot coffee.
For a beer and sausage party, serve a selection of salami and other cooked sausages which you can buy ready to serve. Add any sausage recipes from other sections of this book and the salads and ices suggested for a Pancake party.

PANCAKE PARTIES

A pancake party is good value at any time of year, not just on Shrove Tuesday. It is more unusual than a Wine and Cheese party or a Beer and Sausage party, so a selection of recipes is given below.
For any Pancake party, make up a good quantity of batter; enough to give each person three or four pancakes each. Fry the pancakes shortly before the guests arrive. Stack them flat, one on top of another, with greaseproof paper between them. They re-heat quickly and easily if covered with foil and placed in a very cool oven.
Most fillings can also be made ahead, and re-heated. Make three or four kinds, and keep them warm, or re-heat them in a bain-marie or water bath.
The usual way to serve pancakes is on a side table or buffet. Each guest is given a plate, a pancake, and the filling of his choice, from the selection standing either in a bain-marie or on an electric hot-plate. Salads and ices are refreshing with the main savoury and sweet pancakes.
For all informal parties like this, make

sure that plenty of paper napkins are at hand, to save greasy fingers—and furniture.

PANCAKE BATTER

4 oz plain flour	½ pt milk
1 egg	Salt-pinch

Mix the flour, egg, milk and salt into a smooth batter, let it stand for ½ hr.
To fry, use a small clean frying pan. Rub it with pork or bacon rind and heat until the fat just begins to smoke. Tip in enough batter to coat the bottom of the pan, and swirl the pan to make it do so. Fry until the pancake is set underneath. Lift with a spatula and turn over. Fry the second side very briefly. Keep warm on greaseproof paper until the rest of the pancakes are fried.

SAVOURY PANCAKES WITH BACON

Pancake batter	Dripping
4 bacon rashers	

Whilst the batter is standing for ½ hr, remove the rind from the bacon, cut the bacon into small pieces and fry gently. Remove from frying-pan, draining off the fat, and stir into the batter. Put a little dripping into the frying-pan and heat until smoking hot. Quickly pour in enough batter to coat the bottom of the pan evenly. Cook until brown underneath, turn and brown on the other side. Serve immediately with grilled mushrooms.

4 helpings

SAVOURY PANCAKES WITH CHEESE

1 small onion	4 tablesp milk
4 oz cheese	Salt and pepper
1 oz butter *or* margarine	Pancake batter

Grate the onion and cheese. Put into a

saucepan, add the butter or margarine an stir in the milk. Season to taste. Hea gently until thoroughly hot.
Make the pancakes, spread with the h filling and roll up. Serve immediately.

4 helpings

PANCAKES STUFFED WITH KIDNEYS IN PORT WINE

4 sheeps' kidneys	1 tablesp port
1 small onion or	Salt and pepper
2 shallots	½ pt tomato
1 oz butter *or*	sauce
margarine	Watercress to
¼ pt basic brown	garnish
sauce	Pancake batter

Skin the kidneys and remove the core Soak for 5 min in cold water. Dry, and cu into ¼-in slices. Chop the onion or shallo finely. Heat the fat in a sauté pan, and fr them slightly. Then put in the sliced kid ney and shake and toss over the heat fo about 5 min. Drain off the surplus fat an add the brown sauce, port, salt and peppe Stir over a gentle heat until really hot, bu do not let the mixture boil.
Make the pancakes. Spread with hot fill ing, and roll up. Serve immediately gar nished with watercress, and with tomat sauce in a separate sauce boat.

4 helpings

SAVOURY PANCAKES WITH TUNA AND PRAWNS

1 large green	4–5 oz commer-
pepper	cial soured
1 oz butter	cream
1 oz flour	3 tablesp single
1 7-oz can tuna	fresh cream
fish, flaked	Pancake batter
4 oz prawns, peeled	
Salt and pepper	

Remove the stalk and seeds from th pepper. Cut into ¼-in pieces, and blanch i boiling salted water for 1 min. Drain. Mel the butter, add the flour and cook ove moderate heat for 2 min. Blend in the flaked tuna, the prawns, the blanched pepper, soured and single cream. Stir over gentle heat until hot but not boiling. Season to taste, and keep warm.

Make the pancakes. Heat a little dripping in a frying-pan, pour in enough batter to coat the bottom and shake. Cook until brown, turn and brown the second side. Spread the pancakes with the filling, roll or fold them, and serve while hot.

4 helpings

GRILLED MUSHROOMS

12 flat mushrooms	**Buttered toast**
Salt and pepper	**Chopped parsley**
Butter *or* **bacon fat**	**Lemon juice**

Wash, peel and trim the stalks. Season and brush with melted butter *or* bacon fat. Cook under a hot grill, turning them once. Serve in a hot dish or on rounds of buttered toast, with a sprinkling of chopped parsley and a squeeze of lemon juice. A pinch of very finely chopped marjoram, sprinkled on each mushroom prior to grilling, imparts an excellent flavour.

6 helpings

BAKED TOMATOES

6 tomatoes	**Finely chopped**
A little butter *or*	**tarragon**
margarine	**(optional)**
Salt and pepper	**Browned bread-**
Castor sugar	**crumbs (optional)**

Wash the tomatoes and cut them in halves. Put them in a greased, deep fire-proof dish. Season and sprinkle each with pinch of sugar and a pinch of chopped tarragon, if used. Put a tiny piece of butter on each or cover with a well-greased paper. Bake in a moderate oven (180 °C, 350 °F, Gas 4) until soft—about 20 min.

Alternatively, cut the tomatoes in half horizontally or make crossways cuts in the top of each. Press the cut portion into browned breadcrumbs before baking and top with the butter or margarine.

6 helpings

RICE SALAD

3 oz Patna rice	**Small red** *or*
1–2 tablesp olive	**green pepper**
oil	**(capsicum)**
1–2 tablesp	**2–3 gherkins**
vinegar	**Seasoning**
½ teacup cooked	**1 teasp chopped**
peas	**chives** *or* **onion**
½ teacup cooked	**Watercress**
diced carrots	

Cook the rice in boiling salted water, drain and mix with the oil and vinegar while still hot. The smaller quantity of oil and vinegar gives a fairly dry salad. Add the peas, carrots, finely-chopped uncooked red or green pepper, chopped gherkins, seasoning and chives or onion. Put into a dish and garnish with watercress.

5–6 helpings   *Cooking time—12 min (approx.)*

ORANGE SALAD

4 sweet oranges	**Chopped tarra-**
½ teasp castor	**gon and chervil**
sugar	*or* **chopped mint**
1 tablesp French	
dressing	

Peel the oranges thickly with a saw-edged knife, so that all pith is removed. Cut out the natural orange sections. Place in a salad bowl, sprinkle with sugar. Pour the dressing over and sprinkle with tarragon and chervil, or with chopped mint.

4–6 helpings

CARROT SALAD

3 large carrots	**French dressing**
1 lettuce	**Finely chopped**
	parsley

Grate the carrots finely and serve on a bed of lettuce leaves. Sprinkle with the French dressing. Garnish with chopped parsley. Grated, raw carrot can be used with success in many salads. It should be grated very finely to be digestible, and sprinkled with lemon juice or French dressing as soon as grated to retain its bright colour.

6 helpings

Savoury pancakes with prawns

Lardy cake

COOKED CAULIFLOWER SALAD

1 large cauliflower   Vinaigrette sauce

Steam the cauliflower then divide carefully into small sprigs. Arrange the sprigs neatly in a salad bowl and pour the sauce over while the cauliflower is still warm. Serve when quite cold.

6 helpings

POTATO SALAD

6 large new potatoes *or* **waxy old potatoes**	**1 teasp chopped mint**
French dressing *or* **Vinaigrette sauce**	**1 teasp chopped chives** *or* **spring onion**
2 heaped tablesp chopped parsley	**Salt and pepper**

Cook the potatoes until just soft, in their skins. Peel and cut into dice while still hot. Mix while hot with the dressing and the herbs and a little seasoning. Serve cold.

6 helpings

TOMATO SALAD

6 large firm tomatoes	**French dressing** *or* **cream salad dressing**
Salt and pepper	**Finely chopped parsley**

Skin and slice the tomatoes. Season lightly. Pour the dressing over the tomatoes. Sprinkle with chopped parsley.

6 helpings

Apple pancakes

SWEET PANCAKES

4 oz flour	1 lemon
1 egg	Castor sugar
½ pt milk	A little cooking
Pinch salt	fat

Put about ¼ oz of cooking fat into a cleaned frying-pan and heat until it is just beginning to smoke. Quickly pour in enough batter to coat thinly the bottom of the pan, tilting the pan to make sure that the batter runs over evenly. Move the frying-pan over a quick heat until the pancake is set and browned underneath. Make sure that the pancake is loose at the sides, then toss, or turn with a broad-bladed knife or fish slice. Brown on the other side and turn on to a sugared paper. Sprinkle with sugar and lemon juice, roll up and keep hot while cooking the rest. Serve dredged with castor sugar and pieces of cut lemon.

Other flavourings such as apple, jam, orange, tangerine or brandy may be used, as follows:

Apple pancakes Add grated lemon rind to the batter. Fill with apple sauce mixed with seedless raisins and a little lemon juice.

Jam pancakes Spread with jam before rolling up. Morello Cherry jam is good, topped with whipped cream.

Orange pancakes Make the pancakes, and sprinkle with orange juice and serve with pieces of cut orange.

Tangerine pancakes Add grated tangerine rind to the batter. Sprinkle with tangerine juice before rolling up.

Brandy filling for pancakes Cream together 2 oz butter and 1 oz castor sugar until soft. Work in 1 tablesp brandy and 1 teasp lemon juice. Spread the pancakes with this mixture. Roll up and put immediately into the serving dish.

SYRUP FOR WATER ICES

2 lb loaf sugar	**1 pt water**

Place the sugar and water in a strong saucepan. Allow the sugar to dissolve over gentle heat. Do not stir. When the sugar has dissolved, gently boil the mixture for 10 min, or, if a saccharometer is available, until it registers about 100 °C, 212 °F. Remove scum as it rises. Strain cool and store.

1 pt syrup

LEMON WATER ICE

6 lemons	**1½ pt syrup, as**
2 oranges	**above**

Peel the fruit thinly and place the rind in a basin. Add the hot syrup, cover and cool. Add the juice of the lemons and oranges. Strain, chill and freeze.

6 helpings

LEMON OR ORANGE SORBET

1 pt water	**½ pt lemon** *or*
8 oz loaf sugar	**orange juice**
2 egg whites	

Dissolve the sugar in the water. Boil for 10 min, strain and cool. Add the juice and stiffly whisked egg whites. Freeze and serve at once.

6 helpings

ALFRESCO PARTIES

An alfresco party takes place out of doors, and guests help themselves to food and drinks when they like, either from a long buffet-table or smaller ones. An alfresco party can take place at any time of day—even at breakfast-time—or in the evening.

Once the food is prepared, the hostess's only care need be to see that any hot dishes are kept really hot, and that all the dishes are replenished when required. Dishes which are almost empty look rather forlorn.

SANDWICHES

The term 'sandwich' has a much wider meaning today than when it was first introduced by the Earl of Sandwich, and applied only to slices of meat placed between bread and butter. We have now 'Open' or Continental sandwiches, Club or Two-decker sandwiches, Toasted sandwiches and attractively-shaped Party sandwiches. Their fillings are now immensely varied, savoury or sweet, minced, or shredded and mixed with various butters, sauces and seasonings. Making sandwiches requires little skill, just plenty of imagination and an eye for colour.

For sandwiches the bread should be fresh but not too new; French rolls, Vienna rolls, wholemeal or milk bread make an interesting change from ordinary loaves. Creamed butter is more easily spread than ordinary butter. When ordinary butter is used it should first be beaten to a cream (add 1 teasp hot water to ½ lb butter) to make spreading easier. Savoury butters give piquancy and variety to other fillings, and can be used alone for rolled sandwiches.

Sandwiches simplify entertaining, for they can be prepared well in advance and can be served buffet-style, leaving the hostess free to mix with her guests. If prepared some time before required, sandwiches keep fresh and moist if wrapped in greaseproof paper and then in a damp cloth, or if put into a polythene bag, or wrapped in waxed paper or aluminium foil, and kept in the fridge or a cool place. Sandwiches with different fillings should be wrapped separately to prevent the flavours mixing.

SANDWICH FILLINGS

SAVOURY FILLINGS

1 Anchovies mixed with hard-boiled egg yolk, cheese and butter, with a sprinkling

of cayenne. Spread the bread with curry butter.

2 Canned tuna fish mixed with salad cream, and chopped parsley, with a dash of cayenne.

3 Canned salmon, mashed with lemon juice and chopped chives, spread on a bed of cucumber slices.

4 Minced cooked smoked haddock, seasoned and mixed to a smooth paste with butter and anchovy paste.

5 Very thin slices of cooked chicken and ham, seasoned and placed between bread spread with curry butter.

6 Very finely shredded celery, moistened slightly with canned or double cream, seasoned to taste.

7 Finely grated cheese, mixed to a smooth paste with a little seasoning, anchovy essence or paste, and butter.

8 A layer of finely chopped gherkin, olives and capers, mixed with mayonnaise sauce, covered with a layer of full-fat soft cheese.

9 Mashed sardines, a little lemon juice and seasoning, mixed to a smooth paste with butter.

10 Sardines mashed with an equal amount of grated cheese until smooth; seasoned to taste, with a little lemon juice or vinegar added and sufficient cream or milk to moisten.

11 Minced cooked chicken and ham or tongue, combined with full-fat soft cheese and egg yolk, seasoned and moistened with oil.

12 Finely shredded lettuce and watercress, seasoned with salt and mixed with mayonnaise.

13 Thin slices of Gruyère cheese on slices of bread and butter, spread with French mustard, seasoned with pepper.

14 Slices of hard-boiled egg, seasoned, covered with watercress or mustard and cress, sprinkled with equal quantities of oil and vinegar.

15 Canned foie gras.

16 Minced cooked chicken and ham or tongue, moistened with a little liquid butter and mayonnaise.

17 Lightly spread caviare, sprinkled with lemon juice and a little cayenne. The bread may be spread with shrimp butter.

SWEET FILLINGS

1 Bananas mashed with lemon juice and ground almonds and sprinkled with sugar.

2 A layer of full-fat soft cheese or cottage cheese, covered with a layer of fresh strawberries or raspberries sprinkled with castor sugar.

3 Softened creamed cheese, mixed with canned crushed pineapple and finely chopped preserved ginger.

4 Chocolate spread, mixed with chopped walnuts and cottage cheese.

5 Chopped pears, dates and walnuts, mixed with golden syrup.

6 Thick slices of banana sprinkled with coarsely grated chocolate.

OPEN SANDWICHES

Use ¼-in thick slices of white or brown bread. Spread with softened butter, and with any of the party sandwich fillings below. Garnish with stuffed olives, slices of hard-boiled egg, small pieces of tomato, watercress, piped cream cheese, etc.
The appeal of these sandwiches lies in the artistic way in which the garnish is arranged. They must look colourful, fresh and tempting. Remember that garnishes stay fresher if arranged vertically, and if kept under damp paper or cloth until serving time.

SAVOURY SCANDINAVIAN GARNISHES

1 Samsoe cheese with radish.

2 Tongue with Russian salad, cucumber and a twist of tomato.

3 Egg and crisply fried bacon, with cucumber and a twist of tomato.

4 Liver pâté with mushrooms sautéed in butter, shreds of crisply fried bacon, tomato, lettuce and gherkin.

5 Pork luncheon meat with horseradish cream, and an orange butterfly.

6 Danish blue cheese with black grapes.

7 Salami (without garlic) with raw onion rings and chopped parsley.

8 Pork luncheon meat with young carrots, peas in mayonnaise and cucumber.

9 Danish blue cheese with chopped apple coated with French dressing, topped with a parsley sprig.

Cold table with open sandwiches

CONSOMMÉ ROSÉ

4 raw beetroots	**1 onion**
Sugar	**1 bay leaf**
1 qt vegetable	**1 clove garlic**
water *or* **stock**	**1 clove**
3 carrots	**1 egg white**
1 stick of celery	**Salt and pepper**
1½ lb tomatoes *or*	
1 large can tomatoes	

Scrub and peel the beetroots, slice and sugar them and cook in the water or stock till soft. Then lift them out to be used in salad. Cool the stock, add the other vegetables and spices. Beat the egg white and add to the stock. Bring slowly to simmering point and simmer very gently for 1 hr. Strain through a linen cloth. Season and re-heat. This soup can be served hot or cold. If cold, ¾ oz gelatine should be dissolved in a little stock and added to the whole before cooling.

6 helpings

ROLLMOP HERRINGS

These make a most economical hors-d'œuvre by themselves, and add flavour to a mixed hors-d'œuvres.

6 large herrings	**2 bay leaves**
2 oz kitchen salt	**4–6 small**
1 pt water	**gherkins**
1 pt malt vinegar	**Chillies**
2 large onions	**1 tablesp**
	pickling spice

Clean, bone and fillet the herrings. Mix the salt and water together and put the herrings to soak in this for 2 hr. Lift out of the brine, drain and put into a shallow dish, covering with the vinegar and leaving for several hours. Shred the onions finely. Drain the herring fillets, reserving the vinegar, put 1 tablesp of onion on to each fillet and roll firmly. Secure with small wooden cocktail sticks if possible. Put into jars with bay leaves, gherkins and chillies (use 1 per jar). Pour the vinegar from the dish into a saucepan and boil for a few minutes with the pickling spice. Cool and strain over the herrings. Cover the jars and store in a cool place. They will keep for 2–3 weeks prepared in this way. Note that the herrings are NOT cooked for this dish.

6–12 helpings—or fillets can be divided into halves for part of a mixed hors-d'œuvres

CUCUMBER AND SEAFOOD ROLLS

1 large thin *or*	**Mayonnaise**
2 small thin	**1 2-oz can**
cucumbers	**anchovy fillets**
Oil	**Stuffed olives**
Vinegar	**Parsley**
Seasoning	
1 teacup crab *or*	
lobster meat	

Peel the cucumbers and cut them into 1-in thick slices. Cut out the centre portion, place rings on a dish, and pour over a little oil and vinegar. Season well. Pound the crab or lobster meat or blend in an electric blender. Mix the meat with mayonnaise. Drain the cucumber shapes and fill each cavity with this mixture. Twist a whole anchovy fillet round each and place a slice of stuffed olive on top. Garnish with parsley.

About 10 savouries

LIVER PÂTÉ

1 lb calf's *or* pig's liver *or* the livers from poultry	Pinch of mixed herbs
4 oz very lean ham *or* bacon	A few gherkins (optional)
1 small onion	1–2 hard-boiled eggs (optional)
3 oz butter	A little cream (optional)
Seasoning	Extra butter

Cut the liver, ham and onion into small pieces. Heat the butter in a pan and cook the liver, ham and onion for about 6 min—no longer. Put through a very fine mincer twice to give a very smooth mixture. Add the seasoning, herbs and chopped gherkins or chopped hard-boiled eggs too if wished. For a very soft pâté also add a little cream. Put into a dish and cook for about ½ hr in a moderate oven (170 °C, 350 °F, Gas 4), covering with buttered paper and standing in a dish of cold water to prevent the mixture becoming dry. When the pâté is cooked, cover with a layer of melted butter. Serve cut in slices on a bed of crisp lettuce and accompanied with hot toast and butter.

4–6 helpings

MAKING COLD MOUSSES

A cold savoury mousse makes an excellent first course. It may be made with a custard base alone or have cream added. If it contains cream, avoid a creamy main course. A mousse or soufflé may be made in one big mould or in individual ones. In general, mousses are made with pounded or puréed cooked fish, meat or vegetables usually mixed with a starchy substance or panada, and a liquid thickened with egg yolks, and sometimes with gelatine. The stiffly whipped egg whites may then be added, and the mixture is then poured into the carefully prepared mould or moulds to set.

HAM MOUSSE

½ lb cooked ham	2 tablesp white stock
Salt and pepper	
Grated nutmeg	1 drop cochineal
½ pt rich brown stock *or* consommé	1½ gills cream *or* milk

Liver pâté

½ oz gelatine	1 tablesp chopped mushroom
¼ pt aspic jelly	½ gill firm aspic jelly

Tie a band of stiff paper round a china soufflé dish about 5 in diameter so that it stands about 2 in higher than the dish. Pass the ham twice through the mincer, and sieve it; or blend in an electric blender. Season with salt, pepper and nutmeg. Add the brown stock or consommé which should be well coloured and flavoured with a little tomato paste or purée. Dissolve the gelatine in the aspic, together with the white stock. Colour with cochineal, and add to the ham. Whip the cream lightly, fold it into the mixture. When it is just beginning to set, pour it into the prepared soufflé dish. Allow to set. Add the chopped mushroom to the firm aspic, cold but liquid, and pour over the top of the mould. When set, remove the paper. Serve with green salad.

VOL-AU-VENTS AND PATTIES

Vol-au-vent or patty cases filled with savoury mixtures can be served hot or cold. If a mixture is being put into cold pastry cases, make sure it is quite cold. If, on the other hand, it is being put into hot pastry cases, heat the filling and the pastry separately, and put together at the last minute, so that the filling does not make the pastry soft.

Vol-au-vent cases can be bought uncooked, frozen, or ready to use. They can also, of course, be made at home, using frozen or home-made puff pastry.

To make a Vol-au-Vent Case

Roll out the puff pastry to about $\frac{3}{4}$ in thickness, and with a cutter previously dipped in flour, cut into a round or oval shape as desired. Cut cleanly without dragging or twisting the pastry. Place on a baking-sheet, brush over the top of the pastry with beaten egg. With a smaller, floured cutter cut an inner ring, cutting the pastry to about $\frac{1}{2}$ its depth. Bake in a very hot oven (230 °C, 450 °F, Gas 8). When baked, remove the lid and scoop out the soft inside.

To make Patty Cases

Roll out the puff or flaky pastry to a thickness of $\frac{1}{8}$ in and cut into rounds with a $2\frac{1}{2}$-in or 3-in cutter. Remove the centres from half of these rounds with a $1\frac{1}{4}$-in or $1\frac{1}{2}$-in cutter. Turn the pastry upside down after cutting. Moisten the plain halves and place the ringed halves evenly on top. Prick the centres. Place on a baking-tray and allow to stand for at least 10 min in a cold place. Glaze the ringed halves and the small lids and bake in a very hot oven (230 °C, 450 °F, Gas 8). When baked, remove and scoop out any soft inside part. If liked the cases can be made as vol-au-vent cases (above), using smaller cutters.

SUGGESTED FILLINGS FOR VOL-AU-VENTS AND PATTY CASES

Quantities given are enough to fill 12 medium-sized vol-au-vent cases or about 16 cornet cases (allowing a liberal amount of filling).

Chicken

$\frac{1}{2}$ pt thick sauce made with $\frac{1}{2}$ milk and $\frac{1}{2}$ chicken stock	$\frac{3}{4}$–1 lb diced cooked chicken (approx) Seasoning

Mix together well, and if possible add just 1 tablesp cream.

Mushroom

$\frac{3}{4}$ lb mushrooms	$1\frac{1}{2}$ oz flour
2 oz butter or margarine	Seasoning
$2\frac{1}{2}$ gills milk	Cayenne pepper

Chop the mushrooms into small pieces and toss in the hot butter for a few minutes. Add $\frac{1}{2}$ pt of milk and cook gently for about 10 min. Blend the flour with the other $\frac{1}{2}$ gill milk, add to the mushroom mixture. Season well and boil until smooth and thick. Stir as the mixture cools. If wished add 1 tablesp thick cream. Dust with cayenne pepper when the cases are filled.

Sausage and Apple Filling

2 medium onions, peeled and chopped	2 teasp mixed herbs
	Salt and pepper
1 lb sausage meat	1 beaten egg
2 apples, peeled, cored and chopped	Melted butter
1 tablesp chopped parsley	

Sauté the onions in the butter for 4–5 min. Add sausage meat, apples, parsley, herbs and seasoning, and fry a further 3 min. Cool slightly, and add the beaten egg. Pile on toasted bread or in vol-au-vent or patty cases and bake in a moderate oven (350 °F, Gas 4) for 10–15 min or until just set. Top with toasted bread or a pastry 'hat' if appropriate.

4 savouries

Sardine

1 small can of sardines	2 teasp grated Parmesan cheese
1 tablesp white or tomato sauce	or 1 tablesp grated Cheddar cheese
Salt and pepper	
Few drops of lemon juice	

Remove the bones and mash the sardines. Mix with the white or tomato sauce (if using white sauce, add a few drops of anchovy essence). Season, blend with a few drops of lemon juice and the cheese.

ANGELS ON HORSEBACK'

2 oysters	½ teasp chopped
2 small thin	parsley
slices of bacon	Lemon juice
Paprika or	12 small rounds
cayenne pepper	of fried bread or
teasp chopped	4 slices of toast
shallot or onion	

Beard the oysters, trim the bacon, cutting each piece just large enough to roll round an oyster, season with paprika or cayenne pepper, sprinkle on a little shallot and parsley. Lay an oyster on each, add a few drops of lemon juice, roll up tightly and secure the bacon in position with a fine skewer. Cook in a frying-pan, under the grill or in a hot oven (220 °C, 425 °F, Gas 7) just long enough to crisp the bacon (further cooking would harden the oysters), remove the skewers and serve on the croûtes.

helpings or *12 small savouries*
Cooking time—5–10 min

CREAM' CHEESE FLAN

Short crust pastry,	2 teasp sugar
frozen or using	4 oz full fat
oz flour, etc, if	soft cheese
home-made	¼ teasp grated
oz gelatine	lemon rind
tablesp water	1 tablesp
pt milk	lemon juice
egg yolk	¼ pt cream

Line an 8-in flan ring with the pastry and bake 'blind'. Soak the gelatine in the water for 2–3 min. Heat the milk and dissolve the gelatine in it. Beat together the egg yolk and sugar and add the hot milk. Combine with the cheese, stir in the lemon rind and juice. Cool. Whip the cream and fold into cheese mixture. Pour into baked flan case; chill for 2 hr.

HALIBUT WITH ORANGE AND WATERCRESS SALAD

Four 5–6 oz pieces	Mayonnaise
halibut	1 bunch water-
Seasoning	cress (¼ lb)
lettuce	2 small oranges

Prepare the fillets, season, fold in half and steam for 10–15 min between 2 plates; allow to cool. Shred the outer leaves of lettuce and arrange on a salad dish. Place the cooked fillets on this and coat them evenly with mayonnaise. Garnish with the remaining lettuce, fairly large sprigs of watercress and slices of orange.
Note: Turbot may be substituted for halibut.

4 helpings

BRAISED BEEF IN ASPIC

1½ lb fillet of beef	1¼ pt aspic jelly
previously braised	Cooked peas
1 jar of meat paste	Cooked carrots
French mustard	

It is better to braise the beef the previous day if possible and allow it to become quite cold. Trim into an oblong shape and cut lengthwise into slices. Spread each slice alternately with meat paste and mustard, put the slices together again and press between 2 boards. Set a layer of aspic jelly at the bottom of a cake- or bread-tin and decorate with cooked peas and rings of cooked carrots. Pour on another layer of cold, liquid aspic jelly and allow it to set. Place the prepared beef on top, fill up the mould with aspic jelly and allow to set. Unmould on to an oval dish and decorate with chopped aspic. Serve with an appropriate salad or rice.

6 helpings

COLD CHICKEN, GARNISHED

1 cold boiled	1 pt Béchamel or
chicken or fowl or	Supreme sauce
8 drumsticks	½ pt aspic jelly
1 oz gelatine	6 tablesp bottled
	salad cream

GARNISH—selection of

Cucumber slices	Olive
Pimento, red, cut	Lemon rind
in fancy shapes	Green leek
Mushroom	

Joint the chicken if required. Skin and

Angels on horseback with sausage 'spiral' rolls and cocktail sausages

Halibut with Orange and Watercress

trim the joints, then chill them. Dissolve gelatine in a little hot water, stir into the warm sauce. Add the salad cream. Tammy the sauce (i.e. pass it through a thick cloth), to get a smooth glossy result. When cool enough to be a good coating consistency, coat the chicken. Decorate with the chosen garnish, and allow to set. Coat with cold liquid aspic jelly of a coating consistency, pouring it carefully over each piece with a tablespoon. Serve with a good salad.

A cold chicken can also be attractively garnished simply with a coating of semi-liquid aspic jelly and topped with fruits such as green grapes, apricots or cherries, with tiny pieces of tomato or red pepper and walnuts or almonds.

6 helpings

MIXED VEGETABLE SALAD IN SUMMER, USE

3 large new potatoes	1 tablesp chopped parsley
3 new turnips	1 teasp chopped mint
$\frac{1}{2}$ pt shelled peas	Salad dressing
$\frac{1}{2}$ bunch new carrots	

Cook the vegetables and slice the carrots, potatoes and young turnips. Save some of each vegetable for garnish, and toss the rest in the salad dressing with the herbs. Put the mixture in a suitable dish and garnish with the remainder. Baste with a little French dressing.

nickerbocker glory

Cold chicken garnished with pimento flowers

N WINTER, USE

cauliflower	1 small can of
large carrots	peas
parsnip *or*	Salad dressing
turnips	Watercress *or*
cooked beetroot	fine cress
	A little French
	dressing

Steam the cauliflower, carrots, parsnips or turnips. Divide the cauliflower into sprigs. Dice the carrots, parsnip or turnip, and beetroot, or cut into neat rounds with a cutter. Rinse and drain the peas. Mix all trimmings and uneven pieces of vegetable lightly with salad dressing—include some of the peas. Put this mixture into a dish, preferably oblong in shape. Cover with lines of each vegetable, very neatly arranged and with suitable colours adjoining. Garnish the edges with watercress or fine cress. Baste the surface with French dressing.
For Russian Salad, mix the prepared vegetables with mayonnaise instead of salad dressing.

4–6 helpings

KNICKERBOCKER GLORY

1 pt red jelly	1 pt melba sauce
1 pt yellow jelly	2 oz chopped
1 small can	walnuts
chopped peaches	¼ pt sweetened
1 small can	whipped cream
pineapple	8 maraschino
2 pt vanilla ice	cherries
cream *or* 2 family	
sweet packs	

Make the jellies, allow to set, then whip with a fork. Place small portions of chopped fruit in the bottom of tall sundae glasses. Cover these with 1 tablesp of whipped jelly. Place a scoop or slice of ice cream on top of the jelly. Coat the ice cream with melba sauce. Repeat again with fruit, jelly, ice cream and sauce. Sprinkle with chopped nuts. Pipe with sweetened whipped cream. Place a cherry on top of each.

6 individual glasses

STRAWBERRY CREAM BUNS

Chou pastry using 4 oz flour, etc.
Icing sugar

FILLING

½ pt sweetened double cream fla-voured with vanilla essence *or* **½ pt confectioners' custard**

Pipe out and bake the buns like chocolate profiteroles. Split them, remove any damp parts inside, and dry out. When cold, fill the shells with the cream or custard, with the strawberries embedded in it. Replace the lids, and dust with icing sugar.

CONFECTIONERS' CUSTARD

½ pt milk	**1 oz sugar**
¾ oz cornflour	**½ teasp vanilla**
2 yolks *or* **1 whole egg**	**essence**

Blend the cornflour with the milk, stir in the egg yolks and sugar, and cook over a gentle heat until thick. Beat in the vanilla. Allow to cool.

BARBECUES

At a barbecue, guests grill their own meat on the prepared fire, and season or dress it themselves. Steaks, chops, sausages and spare ribs are the most usual grills served; they are placed on trays, usually on a trestle or similar table not too near the fire. Other things to serve are salt, pepper and pots of mustard, crisp lettuce and tomatoes, home-made breads and butter, and fresh fruit.

The success of a barbecue depends on the weather. Rain can make cooking impossible. If there is a risk of rain, it is wise to have one or two dishes consisting of 'grills' such as gammon steaks and ready-prepared additions such as rice, which can be assembled quickly indoors to make a substantial main course.

GAMMON STEAKS WITH RICE

½ lb rice	**2 eating apples, cored and chopped**
2 tablesp chopped parsley	
Seasoning	**6 oz grated cheese**
2 oz butter	
3 oz white breadcrumbs	**4 thick gammon steaks**
	Parsley

Cook the rice in boiling salted water until tender. Drain, stir in the chopped parsley and seasoning, and keep warm. Grill the gammon steaks, turning them once. While they grill, sauté the breadcrumbs in butter, add the diced apple and cook for 2–3 min. Remove from the heat and stir in half the grated cheese.

Place rice in a serving dish, arrange the gammon steaks overlapping, with apple crumb mixture between each slice, sprinkle with grated cheese and replace under the hot grill for a moment or two. Garnish with parsley.

4 helpings

CUMBERLAND LAMB OR MUTTON PIES

12 oz minced lamb *or* **mutton**	**1 dessertsp chopped parsley**
Short crust pastry using 12 oz flour, etc.	**A pinch of thyme**
	Salt and pepper
1 onion	**A little good stock**
4 oz mushrooms	**Egg** *or* **milk**

Chop and lightly fry the onion. Line 1 small round tins or small saucers with ½ the pastry. Mix together the minced mutton, chopped onion, chopped mushroom, parsley, thyme and seasoning. Divide the mixture between the tins. Add to each a little stock to moisten. Cover with lids made from the rest of the pastry. Brush with egg or milk and bake in a moderate oven (180°C, 350°F, Gas 4) for about 30–45 min.

6 helpings

BASIC MILK BREAD

1 lb plain flour	**2 oz lard** *or* **margarine**
1 teasp salt	
½ oz yeast	**½ pt warm milk (approx)**
½ teasp sugar	**1 egg (optional)**

Mix the salt with the warmed flour, cream the yeast with the sugar. Rub fat into flour and mix with the yeast, milk and egg if used, to a fairly soft, light dough. Beat until mixture is smooth and leaves the sides of

he basin clean. Allow to stand in a warm
lace till twice its original size. Then turn
n to a floured board, knead again not too
eavily but until there are only small holes
ı the dough, and put into the prepared
ns. Put to prove until the dough is well
p the sides of the tin then bake in a hot
ven (220 °C, 425 °F, Gas 7).

–4 loaves   *Cooking time—1 hr*

⸱READ PLAIT

ʟoll risen dough into two strips, each 10 in
ɪng by 5 in or 6 in wide. Cut each strip
▌most to the top in three even-sized pieces
nd plait them as if plaiting hair. Damp
nd seal the ends neatly but firmly and
lace on a greased baking-sheet. Allow to
rove 10–15 min. Brush with egg wash and
lace in a hot oven (230 °C, 450 °F, Gas 8).
⸱ake 20–30 min, reducing heat after first
ɪo min to 200 °C, 400 °F, Gas 6 or 190 °C,
75 °F, Gas 5.

loaves   *Cooking time—20–30 min*

▌HOLEMEAL BREAD

▌ lb wholemeal	1 oz yeast
ɪour	2 oz lard
▌ teasp salt	1¾ pt warm
teasp sugar	water

▌ix salt well with flour and make warm in
▌ large basin. Cream the yeast with the
ɪgar, add the warm water, together with
ıe melted fat, and mix with the flour to an
ʟastic dough. Knead well until smooth,
ɔver with a cloth, to prevent surface
ʋaporation, and set in a warm place to
ɪse to double its size—about 1 hr. When
ıe dough is sufficiently risen it has a
ɔneycombed appearance. The first knead-
ıg distributes the yeast and softens the
▌luten of the flour. Knead the dough a
⸱cond time to distribute the carbonic acid
ɪas which has formed. Continue kneading
ntil, when the dough is cut, there are no
ɪrge holes in it, but do not knead too
▌eavily. Divide into the number of loaves
⸱quired. Place in warmed greased tins,
▌aking the top round. Prick and allow to
⸱rove or recover for 20 min or until the
ɔugh is well up to the top of the tin. If the

dough is over-proved it will collapse and
give heavy bread. Bake in top middle of
a very hot oven (230 °C, 450 °F, Gas 8), for
10–15 min, then reduce heat to fairly hot
(190 °C, 375 °F, Gas 5), baking in all about
1 hr. When ready the loaf should have a
hollow sound when knocked on the bottom,
and should be well risen and nicely
browned with a crisp crust.

4 loaves   *Cooking time—1 hr*

FANCY BREAD ROLLS
(BASIC DOUGH)

½ lb plain flour	1 heaped teasp
1 level teasp salt	castor sugar
1 oz margarine	¼ pt skim milk
½ oz fresh yeast *or*	made from
¼ oz dried yeast	milk powder

Sift the flour and salt into a large bowl.
Leave to stand in a warm place for 10–15
min. Rub in the margarine. Cream the
yeast and sugar together until liquid.
Warm the milk and stir it into the yeast
mixture. Make a well in the centre of the
flour, pour in the liquid and mix to a soft
dough. Knead for 5–10 min on a floured
surface, until the dough is smooth and
glossy. Place in a greased bowl, turn over
to grease the whole surface of the dough,
cover with a damp cloth, and leave to rise
until doubled in size. Shape as required.

Trefoils
Divide the basic dough into 8 pieces, then
divide each piece into 3 bits. Form these
into balls and cluster 3 together in a patty-
tin. Fill 8 tins, then leave in a warm place
until doubled in size. It will take about
15 min. Brush with beaten egg yolk and
skim milk to glaze, and scatter on a few
poppy seeds. Bake in a fairly hot oven, at
200 °C, 400 °F, Gas 6 for 15–20 min.

Bread Knots
Divide the dough into 8 pieces and roll
each into a tube shape about 10-in long.
Tie in a loose knot. Prove and glaze as
above, place on a greased baking-sheet, and
bake like trefoils.

Strawberry cream buns

ue cheese and apple savouries

Baked potatoes in their jackets

aby cottage loaves

ivide the basic dough into 8 pieces. Cut
ach piece into a smaller and larger piece.
hape into rounds. Place the larger rounds
n a greased baking-sheet, and put the
naller ones on top. Make a dip in the
entre of each with your finger. Prove and
aze like trefoils, and bake in the same way.

inger twists

nead 2 level teasp ground ginger into
ae dough (or sift in with the flour).
ivide the dough into 16 pieces and roll
ich out 6-in long. Twist 2 pieces together,
nd place on a greased baking-sheet.
rove, glaze and bake like trefoils. When
oked and cool, brush over with icing
ade from sifted icing sugar and water.

WINTER EVENING PARTIES

Winter evening parties take place *in*doors.
But they can be as informal as alfresco
parties, especially on an occasion like Guy
Fawkes Night when the guests (who include children) spend their time between
the indoor warmth and the scene outside.
The food is, again, served buffet-style, for
guests to help themselves. Any of the dishes
above are suitable, or the hostess can pick
ideas from other sections of this book. But
she should make sure that some really
heart-warming hot dishes are included,
such as the ones which follow here.

97

MULLIGATAWNY SOUP

1 lb lean mutton *or* rabbit *or* stewing veal *or* shin of beef *or* ox tail	1 qt bone stock *or* water
	Salt
1 onion	1 carrot
1 small cooking apple	½ small parsnip
	A bunch of herbs
1 oz butter *or* margarine	Lemon juice
	¼ teasp black treacle
½ oz curry powder	2 oz boiled rice
1 oz flour	

Cut the meat in small pieces. Chop finely the onion and the apple. Heat the butter in a deep pan and in it quickly fry the onion, then the curry powder. Add the apple and cook it gently for a few minutes, then stir in the flour. Add the liquid, meat and salt, and bring slowly to simmering point, stirring all the time. Add the other vegetables, the herbs tied in muslin and a few drops of lemon juice. Simmer until the meat is very tender. This will take between 2 hr for rabbit to 4 hr for shin of beef. Taste the soup and add more lemon juice or add black treacle to obtain a flavour that is neither predominatingly sweet nor acid. Strain the soup, cut some of the meat in neat cubes and reheat them in the soup. Boil, drain and partly dry the rice as for curry and hand it with the soup.
Note: The amount of curry powder may be varied to taste; the quantity given is for a mild-flavoured soup.

4–6 helpings   *Cooking time—from 2–4 hr, according. to the meat used*

POTATOES BAKED IN THEIR JACKETS

6 large potatoes	Butter *or* margarine *or* bacon fat

Scrub the potatoes, rinse and dry them. Brush with melted butter, or margarine or bacon fat or rub with a greasy butter paper. Prick with a fork. Bake on the shelves of a fairly hot oven (190 °C, 375 °F, Gas 5) until soft—about 1½ hr. Turn once whilst they are cooking. Make a cut in the top of each, insert a pat of butter or margarine. Serve in a hot vegetable dish.
New potatoes can be cooked in the same way.

6 helpings

SOMERSET BAKED BACON CHOPS

6 boneless bacon chops	1 large onion
	1 oz butter
1 oz melted butter	

SOMERSET STUFFING

1 medium-sized onion, finely chopped	4 oz white breadcrumbs
	1 tablesp sultanas
½ oz butter	
6–7 oz cooking apples	Pepper
	1 large egg, beaten

Cut through the bacon chops from the outside edge to within ¾ in of the inside edge with a sharp knife, to form a 'pocket'. Fry the onion in butter for 5 min. Peel, core and grate the apples. Mix onion, breadcrumbs, sultanas and pepper together. Bind with the egg. Use this mixture to stuff the 'pockets' in the chops. Place in a roasting tin. Spoon over melted butter and bake in a moderately hot oven (190 °C, 375 °F, Gas 5) for 30 min, basting from time to time, until the chops are golden and tender. Garnish with fried onion rings.
6 helpings   *Cooking time—30 min*

PEASE PUDDING

1½ pt split peas	2 oz butter *or* margarine
1 small onion	
Small bunch of herbs	2 eggs
	Salt and pepper

Soak the peas overnight, remove any discoloured ones. Rinse and cover with cold, salted water. Bring slowly to boiling point in the water, to which has been added the onion (whole) and the bunch of herbs. Simmer very slowly until tender—2–2½ hr. Drain well and rub through a sieve. Add the butter, cut in small pieces, the beaten eggs, pepper and salt. Beat well until the ingredients are well incorporated. Tie tightly in a floured cloth and simmer in water for an hour. Turn out and serve very hot. Pease pudding is served with hot pickled pork and other pork and bacon dishes.

6 helpings

BLUE CHEESE AND APPLE SAVOURIES

3 oz blue-veined cheese, crumbled	Salt and pepper
1 oz butter *or* margarine	2-3 cooking apples
Flour for dredging	Tarragon butter, shaped into
1 oz breadcrumbs	small balls

Cream together the cheese and butter or margarine. Mix in the breadcrumbs, using a fork. Core the apples but do not peel them. Cut each one into 3 or 4 thick rounds. Lay them on a baking-sheet or grilling tray. Season. Dredge with flour to dry, then spread each round with cheese mixture all over. Smooth the surface. Grill under high heat until the cheese bubbles and browns. Leave in a warm place until the apple slices begin to soften. Top each slice just before serving with a small chilled ball of tarragon butter.

SWEET AND SOUR BEEF CASSEROLE

¾ lb stewing steak, cut in 1-in cubes	½ green pepper, sliced
1 tablesp oil	¼ lb button mushrooms, sliced
1 oz seasoned cornflour	
2 tablesp honey	4 prunes, soaked
2 tablesp vinegar	2 tablesp green olives, stoned
¾ pt water	

Preheat the oven to 180 °C, 350 °F, Gas 4. Melt the oil in a 2½-pt freezer-to-table-ware saucepan or casserole and gently fry the beef until the cubes are browned on all sides. Stir in the honey, vinegar and water. Then add the cornflour, blended with water.
Place the pan in the preheated oven and cook for 2 hr. After 1½ hr add the carrots, prunes and olives.
Cool the dish completely and skim off the fat. Cover with a lid and seal with freezer tape. Return to the oven for 45 min.

4 helpings

TURKEY OR CHICKEN TARTLETS

1 onion, finely chopped	10 oz cooked, chopped turkey or chicken
1 oz butter	
1 15-oz can apricot halves	½ teasp Tabasco sauce
2 teasp curry paste	Seasoning to taste
2 teasp lemon juice	4 oz frozen peas
	10 oz shortcrust pastry
¼ soured cream	Beaten egg to glaze

Cook the onion in butter until golden. Add the apricot halves. Simmer for 20 min until reduced to a thick pulp. Thin the curry paste with a little water and add to the apricots with lemon juice. Stir in the soured cream and chopped turkey pieces. Bring to the boil and simmer gently for 10 min. Add the Tabasco sauce, and season to taste. Remove from heat and stir in the peas. Leave covered, to cool.
Make up the pastry in the usual way. Halve the dough and roll out ½. Cut out 5-in rounds to line large individual patty tins. Divide the cooled turkey filling equally between the tarts. Using the remaining pastry, cut out and cover the tarts, glazing with beaten egg to make the edges stick. Pinch the edges together with thumb and forefinger and decorate the tops with pastry 'leaves'. Glaze with beaten egg. Cook for 15–20 min at 220 °C, 425 °F, (Gas 7), or until golden brown. To serve hot, heat at 180 °C, 350 °F, (Gas 4) for 15 min. Cover with greaseproof paper before heating.

Supper Parties

SUPPER 'BEFORE A SHOW'

Pre-theatre and other early evening suppers should be easy and quick to eat. They are intended to sustain one until later in the evening, rather than to be the final meal of the day; and time is usually a factor for people going out to a film, skating session or similar activity.

MINESTRONE

¼ lb haricot beans	2 carrots
3 pt water	1 small turnip
2 onions	2 sticks of celery
1–2 cloves of garlic	2 small potatoes
1 oz lean bacon	½ small cabbage
scraps	2 oz macaroni
2 tablesp olive oil	or fancy shapes
A bunch of herbs	of Italian pasta
2 large tomatoes	Salt and pepper
1 glass red wine	Grated cheese

Soak the beans overnight in ½ pt of the water. Slice the onions, crush the garlic, chop the bacon. Heat the oil in a deep pan and fry the onion very gently for 10 min. Add the garlic, bacon, herbs, cut-up tomatoes and the wine. Reduce this mixture by rapid boiling for 5 min. Add the haricot beans and all the water and simmer for 2 hr. Dice the carrots, turnip and celery and add them to the soup; simmer for a further ½ hr. Add the potatoes, diced, and simmer for another ½ hr. Add the shredded cabbage and the macaroni and simmer for a final 10–15 min. Season the soup, stir into it a little grated cheese and hand the rest round separately. Different mixtures of vegetables may be used when they are in season.

6 helpings

SCAMPI OR DUBLIN BAY PRAWNS PROVENÇALE

8 oz frozen or fresh	2 tomatoes
scampi or Dublin	2–3 large mush-
Bay prawns	rooms
(weight when	Seasoning
peeled)	2 teasp chopped
1 oz butter	parsley
1–2 tablesp olive	Lemon juice
oil	
1 small onion	
½ clove garlic	

Separate frozen scampi. Heat the butter and oil together, then fry the thinly sliced onion, crushed clove of garlic (½ clove is sufficient for most people). Skin and slice the tomatoes, slice the mushrooms and add to the onion with the shellfish and fry together until just tender. Season well,

Boston pork casserole

Minestrone

then add the parsley and lemon juice and serve at once.

For a more substantial dish serve on a bed of boiled rice.

2–3 helpings

DEVILLED CHICKEN LIVERS

4 chickens' livers	**Pinch of salt**
1 shallot *or* **small onion**	**8 small rashers of bacon**
½ teasp chopped parsley	**4 croûtes of fried bread**
Pinch of cayenne pepper	

Wash and dry the livers; cut them in halves. Finely chop the shallot or onion and mix with the parsley, cayenne pepper and salt. Sprinkle this mixture over the livers. Wrap the rashers of bacon round the livers, and fasten them in position with skewers. Bake in a moderate oven (180 °C, 350 °F, Gas 4) for 7–8 min or cook under the grill. Remove the skewers, put 2 bacon rolls on each croûte and serve as hot as possible.

4 helpings

AUBERGINES WITH POACHED EGGS

3 aubergines	**1 tablesp bread-crumbs**
½ oz butter	
¼ pt tomato pulp	**Salt and pepper**
2 tablesp chopped ham	**6 small poached eggs**
	Chopped parsley

Boil the aubergines in slightly salted water until tender, or steam them. Halve them lengthwise, and remove seeds if necessary. Heat the butter, add the tomato pulp, ham, breadcrumbs and stir over heat. Season well, then fill the cavities of the aubergines with the mixture. Put into a greased dish in a moderate oven (180 °C, 350 °F, Gas 4) and heat thoroughly. Place a neatly trimmed poached egg on each half; garnish with parsley and serve.

6 helpings　　　　*Cooking time—about 1 hr altogether*

RISOTTO

4 oz long-grain rice	Salt and pepper
1 small onion	2 tablesp grated Parmesan cheese
2 oz butter	1 pt vegetable stock or water

Wash and dry the rice thoroughly. Chop the onion finely; heat the butter and fry the onion until lightly browned. Then add the rice and fry it until brown. Put in the stock or water, add salt and pepper to taste, boil rapidly for 10 min and afterwards simmer slowly until the rice has absorbed all the liquid. Stir in the cheese, add more seasoning if necessary, then serve.

Alternatively

½ lb long-grain rice	1 teasp salt
2 oz butter	¼ teasp pepper
1 small onion, finely chopped	Stock
½ teasp saffron	1 pt tomato sauce
Nutmeg	2 oz grated Parmesan cheese

Wash, drain and dry the rice thoroughly in a clean cloth. Heat the butter in a saucepan, put in the onion, and when lightly browned add the rice, and shake the pan over the heat for about 10 min. Then sprinkle in the saffron, a good pinch of nutmeg, salt and pepper. Cover with stock, and cook gently for about 1 hr adding meanwhile the tomato sauce and as much stock as the rice will absorb, the sauce being added when the rice is about half cooked. Just before serving stir in the cheese.

This savoury rice is frequently used for borders instead of plainly boiled rice or mashed potatoes.

Either of these recipes can be used as a main dish, accompanied by small bowls of chutney, cooked shrimps, shredded green peppers or canned red pimentos, sliced hard-boiled eggs and other hors-d'œuvre or salad ingredients. Each person can then choose which garnishes he prefers.

2–3 helpings

PEARS FILLED WITH NUT AND DATE SALAD

3 ripe dessert *or* canned pears	2 oz chopped walnuts
1 small crisp lettuce	Chopped parsley
	French dressing
4 oz chopped dates	*or* salad dressing

Peel and halve the pears. Remove the cores with a sharp teaspoon, then scoop out a little of the pulp of the pears to leave a hollow for the filling. Shred a few lettuce leaves very finely and mix with dates, walnuts, chopped parsley and finely diced pear pulp and French dressing *or* salad dressing. Place the halved pears on small crisp lettuce leaves on individual plates. Pile the mixture on each piece of pear. If fresh pears are used, squeeze lemon juice over them to prevent discoloration.

6 helpings

WAFFLES

8 oz plain flour	1 pt milk
¼ teasp salt	2 oz margarine
¾ oz yeast	2–3 eggs
½ teasp sugar	Maple or golden syrup

Sift flour and salt into a bowl. Cream the yeast with the sugar and add to the warm milk and margarine; beat the eggs. Add the yeast, milk and egg to the flour, using more milk if required to make a pouring batter. Set aside to rise for 30–45 min. Heat and grease the waffle iron and pour in enough batter to fill the iron sections—the lid must press on the batter. The waffles are ready when nicely browned. Serve hot with maple or ordinary syrup.

30–40 waffles

APPLE-RAISIN LATTICE TART

Short crust pastry, frozen *or* using 8 oz flour, etc	**4–6 oz sugar, brown *or* white**
¼ lb tart dessert apples	**½ oz flour**
½ lb seedless raisins	**Pinch of salt**
1 tablesp lemon juice	**1 oz butter**

Line a 9-in pie plate with ⅔ pastry, reserving the rest for lattice strips. Peel, core and chop apples, and toss in lemon juice to coat. Mix the fruits, and then mix in any dry ingredients. Turn into the pastry-lined plate. Dot with butter and arrange a lattice of pastry strips over the top. Bake in a very hot oven (230°C, 450°F, Gas 8) for 7–8 min, then reduce heat to moderate (180°C, 350°F, Gas 4) for 30–40 min.

LATE NIGHT PARTIES

A late supper tends to be informal. The food should never be elaborate; it should either be a dish which cooks 'by itself' long and slowly, or is ready beforehand, or one which is easy and quick for the hostess to prepare.

FRENCH ONION SOUP

2 oz fat bacon	**¼ pt white wine *or* cider**
6 medium-sized onions	**6 small slices of bread**
½ oz flour	**2 oz cheese:**
Salt and pepper	**Gruyère *or***
½ teasp French mustard	**Parmesan**
1½ pt stock	**A little butter**

Chop the bacon and heat it gently in a deep pan till the fat runs freely. Slice the onions thinly and fry them slowly in the bacon fat till golden. Add the flour, salt and pepper to taste and continue frying for a few minutes. Stir in the mustard, the stock and the wine or cider. Simmer till the onions are quite soft. Toast the bread, grate the cheese. Butter the toast and spread the slices with grated cheese. Pour the soup into individual fireproof soup bowls, float a round of toast on each and brown it in a very hot oven or under the grill.
This soup can be served either at the beginning or end of a late night party.

6 helpings

FRIED SCAMPI WITH TARTARE SAUCE

8 oz frozen *or* fresh Dublin Bay prawns or scampi (weight when peeled)	**Fat for frying**
	Tartare sauce
	Batter for coating (*see* below)

Separate the frozen prawns or dry the fresh ones. Make the batter. Season well. Dip each prawn in batter and lower into really hot fat. Cook quickly until golden-brown. Drain on crumpled or absorbent kitchen paper. Serve on a hot dish with tartare sauce and serve a plain salad with them.

3–4 helpings

Batter for Coating

4 oz plain flour	**1 egg**
Pinch each of sugar and of salt	**1 gill milk**

Sift together the flour and salt. Make a well in the centre of the flour and add the egg and some of the milk. Mix to a stiff consistency, using more milk if required. Beat well. Add the rest of the milk. Leave to stand for about 30 min.

Aubergines with poached eggs

Waffles with fruit and jam

Pears filled with nuts and dates

French onion soup

TARTARE SAUCE

¼ pt mayonnaise	A little French
1 teasp each of	mustard
chopped gherkin,	1 dessertsp wine
chopped olives,	vinegar
chopped capers,	A little dry white
chopped parsley,	wine (optional)
chopped chives	

Mix the chopped ingredients into the mayonnaise, add the mustard. Thin to the required consistency with the vinegar and wine.

BOSTON PORK CASSEROLE

1 lb dried haricot beans	4 tablesp black treacle
2 medium onions, peeled and thinly sliced	2 level teasp dry mustard
½–¾ lb fat belly of salt pork cut into 1-in cubes	1 level teasp salt Good shake pepper

Wash the beans, cover with water and leave to soak overnight. Drain but keep ½ pt water. Fill a large heat-proof casserole (or traditional bean pot) with beans, onions and pork. Combine the reserved water with the remaining ingredients, pour into casserole, then cover with lid. Cook in the centre of a very slow oven (140 °C, 290 °F, Gas 1) for 5–6 hr. Stir occasionally and add a little more water if beans seem to dry slightly while cooking.

4 helpings

SAVOURY OMELETTES

There are two types of omelette; the French which is flat and generally served folded into three, and the English which is fluffy and more like a soufflé. The essentials in making either type are a thick, clean and dry omelette pan of the right size, i.e. 6–7 in in diameter for a 2- or 3-egg omelette; butter; eggs; and seasonings.

FRENCH OMELETTE

2–3 eggs	½ oz butter
Salt and pepper	

Break the eggs into a basin. Add salt and pepper to taste. Beat the eggs with a fork until they are lightly mixed. Heat the butter in the pan and slowly let it get hot, but not so hot that the butter browns. Without drawing the pan off the heat, pour in the egg mixture. It will cover the pan and start cooking at once.

Shake the pan and stir the eggs with a fork away from the side to the middle. Shake again. In about 1 min the omelette will be soft but no longer runny. Let it stand for 4 or 5 seconds for the bottom to brown slightly. Then remove from the heat. Using a palette knife, fold the omelette from two sides over the middle. Then slip on to a hot dish, or turn it upside down on to the dish.

This omelette can be eaten plain, or it can be filled. There are two methods of filling: flavouring such as herbs, cheese can be added to the eggs after they are beaten, or added to the omelette just before it is folded.

Suggested savoury fillings (quantities given are for 2-egg omelettes)

Cheese: Grate 2 oz hard cheese finely. Add most of it to the mixed eggs, saving a little to top the finished omelette.

Fines Herbes: Finely chop 1 tablesp parsley and a few chives, and add this to the mixed eggs before cooking.

Onion: Sauté a large onion in a little butter but do not get it too greasy. When cool, add to the egg mixture, saving a few hot morsels for garnishing the omelette.

Kidney: Peel, core and cut 2 lamb's kidneys into smallish pieces, and sauté them in a little butter with a small chopped onion or shallot. Pile this mixture along the centre of the omelette after cooking but before folding.

Mushroom: Wash and chop 2 oz mushrooms, sauté them in a little butter until tender. Put them along the centre of the cooked omelette.

Shellfish: Shrimps, prawns, crayfish, lobster or crab, fresh or canned, can be used. Chop if necessary and warm slowly through in a little white sauce so they are hot when the omelette is cooked. Then pile the mixture along the centre.

panish: Make a mixture of chopped ham,
ɔmato, sweet pepper, a few raisins, 1 or 2
ɪushrooms, and sauté in a little butter or
live oil. Add this to the egg before cook-
ɪg; serve this omelette flat.

ɪNGLISH OMELETTE

eparate the eggs. Add half an egg-shell of
ʋater for each egg to the yolks: beat them
ʋith a wooden spoon until creamy. Whisk
ɪe whites until they stay in the basin
ʋhen turned upside down. Gently fold the
ʋhites into the yolks. Have the butter
eady in the pan as for the French Ome-
ɪtte. Pour in the egg mixture, and cook
ntil it is golden-brown on the underside.
ʼhen put the pan under the grill and lightly
ɪrown the top. Fillings are usually spread
ʋer the cooked omelette. Now run a palette
ɪnife round the edge of the pan. Fold the
ɪmelette over and slip on to a hot dish.

ʋELSH RAREBIT

oz butter *or*	A few drops of
ɪnargarine	Worcester sauce
level tablesp	4–6 oz grated
lour	Cheddar cheese
tablesp milk	Salt and pepper
ʳ 3 tablesp milk	4 slices of
nd 2 tablesp	buttered toast
le *or* beer	
teasp mixed	
ɪustard	

Ieat the fat in a pan and stir in the flour.
ɪook for several minutes, stirring-well. Add
ɪe milk and stir well over the heat until a
ɪmooth thick mixture, then add the ale,
ɪustard, Worcester sauce, cheese and a
ood pinch of salt and pepper. Do not
ʋercook the mixture otherwise the cheese
ʋill become 'oily'. Spread on the slices of
ɪuttered toast and put under a hot grill
ɪntil golden-brown. Serve at once.
ɪ larger quantity of Welsh Rarebit mix-
ɪure can be made and stored in the fridge
ɔ be used as required.

helpings or *8 small savouries*

GRILLED KIDNEYS

6 sheeps' kidneys	Salt and pepper
Oil *or* oiled butter	Croûtes of fried bread

GARNISH

Maître d'Hôtel butter *or* **bacon rolls**

Prepare the kidneys as directed in the preceding recipe and keep them open and flat
with a skewer. Brush with oil or melted
butter and season with salt and pepper.
Grill quickly, cooking the cut side first and
turning frequently. When ready, remove
the skewer and serve on croûtes of fried
bread on a hot dish. The hollow in the
centre of the kidney may be filled with a
small pat of Maître d'Hôtel butter, or the
dish can be served with rolls of bacon.

6 helpings   *Cooking time—5–8 min*

LEMON MERINGUE PIE

**Rich shortcrust pastry,
using 8 oz flour, etc**

FILLING

2 eggs	2 level teasp
8 oz can sweetened	cream of tartar
condensed milk	1 lemon
2 oz castor sugar	

Make the pastry and line an 8- or 9-in pie
plate. Bake it 'blind'.

To make the filling Separate the egg
yolks from the whites. Beat the yolks until
thick and lemon coloured. Fold in the con-
densed milk, lemon rind, juice and cream
of tartar. Pour into the baked pie shell.
Spread with meringue made from the egg
whites and the sugar. Decorate lightly
with cherries and angelica. Bake in a cool
oven (100 °C, 200 °F, Gas ½) for ½–1 hr.

Coffee and Tea Parties

BASIC PLAIN SCONES

1 lb plain flour	**2–3 oz lard** *or*
½ teasp salt	**margarine**
and	

2 level teasp bicarbonate of soda and 4½ level teasp cream of tartar with ½ pt fresh milk

or

2 level teasp bicarbonate of soda and 2 level teasp cream of tartar with ½ pt sour *or* **butter milk**

or

4–6 level teasp baking-powder with ½ pt fresh milk

Sift flour and salt and lightly rub in the fat; sift in the raising agents and mix well. Add *all the milk at once* and mix *lightly* to a *spongy* dough. Knead very lightly to make the dough smooth and roll out ½–¾ in thick. Cut out with a 2-in cutter, brush with egg *or* milk if desired, and bake in a hot oven (220–230 °C, 425–450 °F, Gas 7–8). If you prefer, the dough can be divided into 4 and each piece formed into a round cake and marked into 6 with a knife.

24–30 scones   *Cooking time—about 10 min*

VARIATIONS OF BASIC RECIPE

Cheese scones
Add 4–6 oz grated cheese to the dry ingredients above. Cut out in finger shapes or squares.

Cheese whirls
Add 4–6 oz grated cheese to the basic recipe. Roll out dough into oblong shape. Spread with cheese and roll up like a Swiss Roll. Cut into slices and lay on greased baking-sheets with the cut side uppermost. Brush with milk or egg. If any cheese is left over, sprinkle it on and bake the whirls in a hot oven (220–230 °C, 425–450 °F, Gas 7–8).
20–24 scones   *Cooking time—10–15 min*

Fruit scones
Add 2 oz sugar and 2–4 oz fruit (currants, sultanas, etc) to the basic recipe.

Griddle scones
Add 2–3 oz currants; roll out ¼ in thick, cut into 2½-in rounds or triangles; cook on both sides on a moderately hot griddle about 5 min till nicely brown and edges dry. Cool in a towel.

A table set for the 'traditional' English tea

Nut scones
Add 2–4 oz chopped nuts to the basic or to the wholemeal recipe.

Sweet scones
Add 2 oz sugar and, if liked, 1 egg.

Treacle scones
Add 1 oz sugar, 1 teasp ground cinnamon, 1 teasp mixed spice, 2 tablesp black treacle. Put the treacle in with ⅔ of the milk, then add the rest as required.

Wholemeal scones
Use half wholemeal flour and half plain flour.

LARDY CAKE

1 lb white bread dough which has risen once	**4 oz currants** *or* **sultanas**
6 oz lard	**A little spice, if liked**
6 oz granulated sugar or a little less	**Sugar syrup to glaze**

Roll out the dough on a floured board, and put on half the lard in dabs, to cover ⅔ of the surface, as in making flaky pastry. Sprinkle with the sugar, fruit and spices to your taste. Fold the dough into

3, folding the unlarded piece over first. Turn to the right, and repeat the sugaring, larding and folding. Turn to the right again, and roll once more. Fold again. Roll, this time to fit a Yorkshire pudding-tin about 12 × 7 in. Put to rise in a warm place, and cover with a clean tea towel. Due to the sugar, it will take longer than usual, but need only rise half its height. This will take about ¾ hr.

Bake in the centre of the oven at 200 °C, 400 °F, Gas 6 for about ¾ hr, until brown and crisp. When cooked (or before), brush with a thick sugar syrup to give a glistening top.

1 The cake looks better if you score the top with a sharp knife into diamond shapes before putting it to rise.

2 It is better eaten hot.

3 This is a traditional recipe, which used to be made on the day bread was baked, or from a piece of dough kept in the cold larder until the next day.

BATH BUNS

1 lb plain flour	**Good ½ oz yeast**
½ teasp salt	**3 oz sugar**
3 oz fat (margarine and lard)	**2 eggs**
	1½–2 gills warm milk

SUGAR SYRUP GLAZE

1 tablesp water	**1 dessertsp sugar**

Mix salt with warmed flour and rub in fat. Mix in most of the sugar. Mix to a light dough with yeast creamed with remainder of sugar, egg, and milk. Put to rise till double its size, then knead lightly. Divide into 24 pieces and shape each 3½–4 in long and 1 in wide. Place fairly close together (so that they join up in baking) on greased baking-sheets and prove 15 min. Bake in a hot oven (220 °C, 425 °F, Gas 7) 10–15 min. To make the glaze—boil together the water and sugar until slightly syrupy. Brush the buns immediately they come from the oven so that the syrup dries on.

Dredge thickly with castor sugar. Break buns apart before serving.

Note: 2 oz sultanas and 1 oz chopped pe can be worked into the dough after it h risen.

24 buns   *Cooking time—10–15 m*

CHELSEA BUNS

½ lb plain flour	**½ oz currants** *or*
¼ teasp salt	**sultanas**
1 oz lard *or*	**½ oz chopped**
margarine	**candied peel**
½ oz yeast	**1 oz sugar**
1 gill warm milk	

Mix flour and salt; rub in fat; cream yea and add to flour, with warm milk. Be well and put to rise to double its siz Knead risen dough lightly and roll out a square of about 10 in. Sprinkle with t fruit and sugar and roll up like a Sw roll. Cut roll into 9 pieces and put cut si uppermost. Place buns in a greased 8-sandwich cake-tin so that they will jo together when cooked and allow to pro till up to the top of the tin. Brush wi milk or egg. Bake in a hot oven (220 °C 425 °F, Gas 7) for 20–25 min. Whe cooked, glaze and dust with sugar li Bath Buns.

9 buns   *Cooking time—20–25 m*

PLAIN BUNS or COOKIES BASIC RECIPE

(Self-raising flour can be used for any the following, in which case omit the rai ing agent.)

1 lb plain flour	**3 teasp baking-**
¼ teasp salt	**powder**
4–8 oz margarine	**2 eggs**
or **lard**	**1–1½ gills milk** *o*
4 oz sugar	**enough to make**
Flavourings as	**a stiff consis-**
below	**tency**

Sift flour and salt into bowl, cut in fat wi round-bladed knife, then rub with finge tips till quite fine. Add sugar and bakin powder. Mix with egg and milk to a sti consistency. (The fork with which the bu are mixed should stand up in the mixture Divide into pieces and form into rock caps on a greased baking-sheet. Bake in hot oven (220 °C, 450 °F, Gas 8–7) until springy and browned.

24–32 buns   *Cooking time—10–15 min*

VARIATIONS OF BASIC RECIPE

Chocolate Buns
Add 1–1½ oz cocoa to the flour and 1 teasp vanilla essence with the milk.

Coconut Buns
Mix in 4 oz desiccated coconut with the sugar.

Ginger Buns
Add 2 small teasp ground ginger to the flour and add 4 oz chopped or grated crystallised ginger with the sugar.

Lemon Buns
Add 1 teasp lemon essence with the milk. Turn mixture on to floured board and make into a roll. Divide into 24 pieces, form into balls, brush with egg *or* milk and sprinkle with coarse sugar.

London Buns
Add 2 oz chopped peel and 2 teasp grated lemon rind when adding the sugar and form mixture into balls as for lemon buns. Glaze and sprinkle with coarse sugar. Place 2 pieces of lemon *or* orange peel on top of each bun.

Nut Buns
Add 4 oz chopped nuts when adding the sugar.

Raspberry Buns
Form basic mixture into 24 balls, make a hole in each bun and place a little raspberry jam in the hole. Close the opening, brush with milk *or* egg and sprinkle with coarse sugar.

Rock Buns
Add 4–6 oz currants and 2 oz chopped peel when adding the sugar.

Seed Buns
Add 2 dessertsp caraway seeds with the sugar.

SCOTTISH SHORTBREAD

8 oz flour	4 oz butter
4 oz castor sugar	

Put the flour and sugar in a pile on a pastry-board. Gradually knead the sugared flour into the butter with the hand. It is important not to let the butter become broken up. When a firm dough is formed, roll out and shape into a cake about 1 in high. Decorate the edges by marking with a fork or fluting with finger and thumb, or make in a shortbread mould, and prick a pattern on top with a fork or skewer. Fasten a narrow band of paper round to keep the cake in shape. Bake in a warm to cool oven (170–150 °C, 325–300 °F, Gas 3–2). Dredge with castor sugar when cooked.

Cooking time—about 1 hr

SCANDINAVIAN TEA RING

6 oz plain flour	Small ½ oz yeast
¼ teasp salt	½–¾ gill warm milk
½ oz sugar	½–1 egg

FILLING

1 oz ground almonds	Hot water to mix to a spreading consistency
1 oz castor sugar	

ICING

3 oz sifted icing sugar	Warm water to mix

DECORATION

½ oz blanched and chopped almonds

Mix flour and salt; add most of the sugar. Cream yeast with remainder of sugar, add warm milk and egg and mix with flour to a light but workable dough. Put the dough to rise and when well risen roll out in an oblong shape. Spread with the almond mixture; damp edges with water and roll up. Form into a ring or horseshoe shape; prove 10–15 min. Bake in a hot oven (220 °C, 425 °F, Gas 7), reducing the heat after 10 min to fairly hot (190 °C, 375 °F, Gas 5). When cold, spread with icing and sprinkle with chopped almonds.

Cooking time—20–30 min

Orange sandwich cake

BASIC LARGE RICH CAKE
A 7-in CAKE

6 oz butter *or* **margarine**	**⅛ teasp salt**
6 oz castor sugar	**2 level teasp baking-powder**
3 eggs	*or* **other raising**
8 oz plain flour	**agents**
Milk to mix	

Line a 7-in cake-tin with greaseproof paper or foil, greased, or with silicone-treated paper. Cream the fat, add the sugar gradually and beat until white and fluffy. Beat in the eggs, one at a time, making sure each is blended in thoroughly before adding the next. Sift in a little of the flour if the mixture shows any signs of curdling. Sift in the flour, salt and baking-powder gradually, and stir in lightly with a spoon. Add enough milk to make a fairly soft batter. Turn into the cake-tin, and bake at 180 °C, 350 °F, Gas 4 for 1–1½ hr or until the cake is springy and brown on top.
If you want to use any of the variations below containing dried fruit, add the eggs

to the creamed mixture, alternately wit the flour divided into 3 parts. Probably n other liquid will be needed, and the cak will be close-textured enough to hold th fruit.

VARIATIONS OF BASIC RECIPE
Cherry Cake
Add 4 oz chopped glacé cherries whe adding the flour.
Fruit Cake
Add 6–8 oz sultanas, currants, raisins o dates to basic mixture. Add eggs and flou alternately. Stir in fruit mixed with som of the flour *after* eggs have been added.
Ginger Cake
Sift ½ teasp ground ginger with the flour add 2–4 oz coarsely chopped crystallise ginger with the flour.
Lemon Cake
Add the grated rind of 2 lemons with th flour. The cake can be iced when col with lemon glacé icing.
Madeira Cake
Add the grated rind of 1 lemon with th flour. Place 2 strips of candied citron pee on top of the cake when mixture has begu to set (after about 30 min).
Seed Cake
Add 2 teasp caraway seeds with the flour

RICH CAKES—SMALL

Use the mixture on page 65 for all thes small cakes and variations. It is repeate here for your convenience.

BASIC RECIPE

2 oz butter *or* **margarine**	**3 oz self-raising flour** *or* **3 oz**
2 oz castor sugar	**plain flour and**
1 egg	**1 level teasp baking-powder**
	Pinch of salt
	Water *or* **milk as required**

Beat the fat and sugar until creamy an white. Whisk the egg and add gradually beat well between each addition. Sift to gether the flour, salt and baking-powder Gently stir flour, etc., into creamed fat

Mocha biscuits

add milk *or* water to make a soft dropping consistency (water is considered best). Half-fill greased bun-tins with the mixture and bake in a fairly hot to moderate oven (190–180 °C, 375–350 °F, Gas 5–4).
Note: This mixture may be baked in paper cases and decorated with glacé icing or cherries.

10–12 cakes   *Cooking time—15–20 min*

VARIATIONS OF BASIC RECIPE

Cherry Cakes
Add 1–2 oz coarsely chopped glacé cherries with the flour.

Chocolate Cakes
Sift ½ oz cocoa with the flour, and add a few drops of vanilla essence with the water or milk. The cakes may be iced with chocolate glacé icing.

Coconut Cakes
Add ½ oz coconut with the flour and add ¼ teasp vanilla essence with the milk or water.

Lemon Cakes
Add the grated rind of 1 lemon with the flour, and ice with lemon glacé icing.

Madeleines
Bake the basic mixture in greased dariole moulds. Turn out when baked; cool. Spread all round top and side with warmed apricot jam. Roll in desiccated coconut, decorate with ½ glacé cherry.

Nut Cakes
Add 1–2 oz coarsely chopped walnuts, almonds, etc, with the flour.

Queen Cakes
Add 1–2 oz currants *or* sultanas with the flour or a few currants may be placed in the bottom of each queen cake-tin and the mixture placed on top.

VICTORIA SANDWICH

4 oz butter *or* **margarine**	**4 oz plain flour**
	Pinch of salt
4 oz castor sugar	**1½ level teasp**
2 eggs	**baking-powder**

Cream fat and sugar very thoroughly. Add well-whisked eggs gradually, beating well between each addition—if sign of curdling, add some flour. Sift flour, salt and baking-powder and stir lightly into the creamed fat and eggs. Mix to a soft dropping consistency, adding a little water if necessary. Place the mixture in a prepared 7-in sandwich-tin and bake in a moderate oven (180 °C, 350 °F, Gas 4).

Cooking time—40–45 min

DUNDEE CAKE

7 oz butter *or* margarine	3–4 eggs
7 oz castor sugar	1 level teasp baking-powder
¾ lb plain flour	Milk *or* water as required
¼ teasp salt	
12–16 oz mixed fruit—currants, raisins, sultanas	Blanched almonds

Line a 7–8-in cake-tin with greaseproof paper. Cream the fat and sugar till light. Sift together flour and salt and mix the fruit with a small amount of the flour. Add the eggs and flour alternately to the creamed fat, beating well between each addition. Mix baking-powder with the last lot of flour, stir in the fruit and if necessary add a little milk *or* water to make a heavy dropping consistency. Put into the cake-tin, make a slight depression in the centre and spread some split blanched almonds over the surface. Bake in a moderate oven (180 °C, 350 °F, Gas 4), reduce heat after ¾ hr to warm to cool (170–150 °C, 325–300 °F, Gas 3–2).

Cooking time—2½ hr

LEMON OR ORANGE SANDWICH CAKE

1 Victoria sandwich cake	Crystallised lemon *or* orange slices
Lemon *or* orange-flavoured butter icing	

Cut cake through the centre and spread with flavoured butter icing. Sandwich

together again. Spread the top of the cake with icing, smooth with a knife and finall decorate with slices of crystallised fruit.
A more pronounced flavour may be ob tained by adding the finely grated rind o 1 lemon or orange when mixing the cak

BASIC LARGE SPONGE CAKE

4 oz plain flour	4½ oz castor suga
Pinch of salt	Grated lemon
3 eggs	rind

Grease and dust a 6-in tin with 1 teasp flou and 1 teasp castor sugar mixed togethe Sift the flour and salt. Beat the eggs an sugar over a pan of hot water till thick an creamy. Fold flour, salt and lemon lightl into the egg and turn the mixture into th tin. Bake in a warm oven (170 °C, 335 ° Gas 3). When cold, split the sponge an spread with jam. Dust with icing sugar.

Cooking time—45 m

MOCHA BISCUITS

5 oz butter	1 tablesp liquid coffee essence
2 oz castor sugar	
7 oz self-raising flour	Beaten egg
½ level teasp powdered cinnamon	

Cream the butter and castor sugar togethe until light and fluffy. Sift the flour an cinnamon and add to the butter and suga together with the coffee essence. Work to gether. Using a forcing bag and rosett pipe, press out round and finger shapes o a greased baking-sheet. Brush with beaten egg. Bake in a moderate oven (180 °C 350 °F, Gas 4) for 25 min or until golden brown.

BANBURY CAKES

Rough puff pastry using 8 oz flou etc, *or* puff *or* flaky pastry may b used

FILLING

Small 1 oz butter *or* margarine	4 oz currants
½ oz plain flour	½ oz chopped candied peel

¼ nutmeg (grated)	2 oz brown sugar
or ¼ teasp ground	2 tablesp rum
cinnamon	

GLAZE

| Egg white | Castor sugar |

To make the filling: melt the fat, stir in the flour and spice and cook for a minute or two. Remove from the heat, add the fruit, sugar and rum.

Roll the pastry out ¼ in thick and cut into 3-in rounds. Place a spoonful of filling in the centre of each, damp the edges and gather them together to form a ball; turn over so that the smooth side is uppermost. Roll each out and shape into an oval shape 4 in by 2½ in; make 3 cuts in the centre. Put the cakes on a greased tin and bake in a hot oven (220 °C, 425 °F, Gas 7). Brush with the egg white and dust immediately with castor sugar. Return to the oven for a few minutes, to frost the glaze.

14 cakes   *Cooking time—20 min*

CRUNCHIES

| 4 oz butter *or* margarine | 1 tablesp golden syrup |
| 2½ oz sugar | 5 oz rolled oats |

Melt fat, sugar and syrup in a saucepan and stir in the oats. Spread on a greased baking-sheet with a raised edge, 7 in by 13 in to within ½ in of the edge. Place in a moderate oven (180 °C, 350 °F, Gas 4) and bake until a good brown colour and firm. Cut into fingers before completely cold.

16 crunchies   *Cooking time—20–30 min*

SMALL ICED OR FRENCH CAKES

| One oblong Genoese pastry cake, 1–1½ in thick Filling of your choice: jam, lemon curd, confectioners' custard *or* butter icing | Cake decorations: chopped nuts, crystallised violets, rose petals, silver balls, glacé fruits, angelica, etc Glacé icing |

Cut the cake through the centre, spread it thinly with filling and join together again. If necessary, trim off the brown top of the cake, and brush off any loose crumbs. Cut the cake into rounds, triangles, squares, etc. Brush off loose crumbs carefully, and put the pieces of cake on an icing rack over a large flat dish.

Make the icing so that it will flow easily over the cakes but will not run right off. Pierce each cake in turn with a skewer, spear it, and dip it into the icing. Return it to the rack, and dislodge the skewer with a fork, so that you do not leave fingermarks on the cake. Once or twice, you can change the colour of the icing, say from white to pale pink to darker pink. Before the icing sets, arrange a little decoration on the top of each cake. When firm, serve the cakes in decorative paper cases.

About 24 cakes

VANILLA SLICES

| Puff pastry, using 3 oz flour, etc | A little glacé icing |

FILLING

½ pt milk	1 oz sugar
¾ oz cornflour	½ teasp vanilla
2 egg yolks *or* 1 whole egg	essence

Roll pastry ½ in thick and cut into fingers 4 in by 1 in. Bake in a fairly hot oven (220 °C, 425 °F, Gas 7) until pastry is well risen. Allow to cool.

Blend the cornflour with the milk, beat in the egg yolks and sugar, and cook over a gentle heat until thick. Beat in the vanilla. Allow to cool.

Slit carefully through the centre of the pastry fingers, spread the custard over one half and sandwich the halves together again. Spread tops thinly with glacé icing.

8 slices   *Cooking time—20 min*

BATTENBURG CAKE

| 2 Victoria sandwich cakes made in oblong tins, one white and the other coloured pink |

Coffee walnut cake

COFFEE WALNUT CAKE

4 oz margarine	4 oz self-raising
4 oz castor sugar	flour
2 eggs	2 oz chopped
1 tablesp coffee	walnuts
essence	Coffee glacé
	icing

Cream together the margarine and castor sugar until light and fluffy. Gradually add the beaten eggs, beating well between additions. Stir in coffee essence and fold in sifted flour, together with chopped walnuts. Turn mixture into a deep 7-in sandwich-tin, well greased, and bake at 190 °C, 375 °F, Gas 5 for 25–30 min. Cool on a rack. Decorate with Coffee Glacé Icing and walnuts.

1 tablesp apricot glaze
Almond paste, using 3 oz ground almonds, etc

DECORATION

Glacé cherries   **Angelica**

Cut the cake into strips 8–9 in long and $1\frac{1}{2}$ in square at ends—2 pink and 2 white pieces will be needed. Join these together with apricot glaze to make a block $9 \times 3 \times 3$ in, with a pink and a white strip side by side, topped with a white strip and a pink one, respectively.
Roll almond paste into an oblong, wide enough and long enough to wrap round the cake leaving the ends open. Trim edges of almond paste. Spread top of cake with apricot glaze and invert on to almond paste. Spread the remaining three sides with glaze, roll up firmly and join almond paste neatly. To decorate, pinch the two top edges between thumb and forefinger. Mark the top of the cake lattice fashion with a knife and decorate with cherries and angelica.

Basic Recipes

These foundation recipes provide products used in many of the dishes above.

SHORT AND RICH SHORT CRUST PASTRY FOR PIES, TARTS, ETC

FOR STANDARD SHORT CRUST PASTRY

½ lb plain flour	2 oz lard
Pinch each of sugar and salt	Cold water to mix
2 oz butter *or* margarine	

Sift the flour, sugar and salt together. Rub the fats into the flour, using only the finger-tips. Mix to a stiff paste with cold water.

FOR RICH SHORT CRUST PASTRY

½ lb plain flour	1 teasp castor sugar
4–6 oz butter (sweet type, if possible)	Cold water to mix (about 1 tablesp)

Make as above, on a flat surface rather than in a bowl. Before adding water, make a well in the dry ingredients, and put in the egg yolk. Sprinkle with the sugar, and mix with the finger-tips or a knife. Add the water as required, and mix.

PÂTÉ SUCRÉE

8 oz plain flour	2 oz sugar
Pinch of salt	1 egg yolk
5 oz butter	Cold water to mix

Sift together the flour and salt. Cut the butter into small pieces and rub it lightly into the flour using the finger tips. Add the sugar and mix with egg yolk and sufficient cold water to make a stiff paste. Use as required.

In warm weather only a very small quantity of water will be required.

CRUMB PASTRY

Crumb pastry can provide a useful short cut to making a tart shell or pie crust. It is made with breadcrumbs, toast or biscuit crumbs or cornflakes. The materials are crushed by hand, wrapped in a cloth and rolled with a rolling-pin, or are processed in an electric blender. As a rule, 6 oz crumbs combined with 3 oz melted butter is used, with sugar and spice flavouring to your taste. This should make a shell for an 8-in plate tart. Mix the crumbs together with the butter well, and press firmly into the bottom and sides of the plate. Either chill, and then fill with a custard or firm fruit purée; or chill and then bake 'blind' at 180 °C, 350 °F, Gas 4, for 15 min.

Fatty crumbs may need less butter, wholemeal stale breadcrumbs may need a little more. A luxury crust can be obtained by using ginger-snaps for the crumbs, or the following mixture:

1½ cups digestive biscuit crumbs	¼ cup thin cream
6 tablesp unblanched ground almonds	½ cup melted butter
	⅛ teasp cinnamon

PUFF PASTRY

(For pies, tarts, tartlets, etc)	
1 lb plain flour	1 teasp lemon juice
Pinch of salt	
1 lb butter	⅛ pt cold water (approx)

Sift the flour and salt and rub in about 2 oz of butter. Press the remaining butter firmly in a floured cloth to remove the moisture, and shape into a flat cake. Add the lemon juice to the flour and mix to a smooth dough with cold water. The consistency of the dough must be the same as that of the butter. Knead the dough well and roll it out into a strip a little wider than the butter and rather more than twice its length. Place the butter on one half of the pastry, fold the other half over and press the edges together with the rolling-pin to form a neat parcel. Leave in a cool place for 15 min to allow the butter to harden. Roll out into a long strip 3 times the original length but the original width, keeping the corners square and the sides straight to ensure an even thickness when the pastry is folded. Do not let the butter break through the dough. Fold the bottom third up and the top third down, press the edges together with a rolling-pin and half turn the pastry so that the folded edges are on the right and left. Roll and fold again and lay aside in a cool place for 15 min. Repeat this process until the pastry has been rolled out 6 times. The rolling should be done as evenly as possible and the pastry kept in a long narrow shape which, when folded, forms a square. Roll out as required and leave in a cool place before cooking.

Bake in a very hot oven (230 °C, 450 °F Gas 8). The oven door should not be opened until the pastry has risen and become partly baked, as a current of cold air may cause the pastry to collapse.

BASIC BROWN SAUCE

1 small carrot	1 oz flour
1 onion	1 pt brown stock
1 oz dripping	Salt and pepper

Thinly slice the carrot and onion. Melt the dripping and in it slowly fry the onion and carrot until they are golden-brown. Stir in the flour and fry it even more slowly till it is also golden-brown. Stir in the stock, bring to simmering point, season, then simmer for ½ hr. Strain the sauce before use. As the frying of the flour is a long process extra colour may be given to the sauce by adding a piece of brown onion skin, or a little gravy browning or a little meat or vegetable extract which will also add to the flavour.

Cooking time—40 min–1 h

BASIC WHITE SAUCE

FOR A COATING SAUCE

2 oz butter *or* margarine	vegetable to suit dish), *or* a
2 oz flour	mixture of stock
Pinch of salt	and milk
1 pt milk *or* stock (fish, meat *or*	

FOR A POURING SAUCE

1½ oz butter *or* margarine	
1½ oz flour	for coating sauce
1 pt of liquid as	Pinch of salt

Melt the fat in a deep saucepan, large enough to hold the amount of liquid with just enough room to spare for beating the sauce. Stir the flour into the fat and allow it to bubble for 2–3 min over a gentle heat. On no account allow it to change colour; this is a white roux. Remove from heat and stir in ½ the liquid gradually. Return to moderate heat and stir the sauce briskly ntil it thickens, then beat it vigorously. eason and use it at once. If the sauce ust be kept hot, cover it with wet grease-roof paper and a lid, and before use eat it again in case skin or lumps have ormed.

coating sauce should coat the back of ne wooden spoon used for stirring, and hould only just settle to its own level in the an.

A pouring sauce should barely mask the poon; it should flow freely, and easily settle o its own level in the pan.

or melted butter sauce, whisk in 2 xtra oz butter, a nut at a time, just before erving.

Cooking time—15 min

BÉCHAMEL SAUCE

pt milk	Salt
small onion	6 peppercorns
small carrot	A small bunch
-in celery stick	of herbs
bay leaf	2 oz butter
clove	2 oz flour
blade of mace	$\frac{1}{8}$ pt cream (optional)

Warm the milk with the vegetables, herbs, alt and spices, and bring it slowly to sim-nering point. Put a lid on the pan and tand it in a warm place on the cooker to nfuse for $\frac{1}{2}$ hr. Strain the milk, melt the utter, add the flour, cook this roux for a ew minutes without browning it. Stir the lavoured milk gradually into the roux. Bring the sauce to boiling point, stirring igorously. For an extra smooth result, vring the sauce through damp muslin. If ream is used, add it to the sauce just at oiling point and do not reboil it. Serve with chicken, veal, fish or white egetables.

Note: Béchamel sauce may be made with white stock and $\frac{1}{2}$ milk, the result will ave a good flavour but will not be so reamy in texture.

Cooking time—40 min

DEMI-GLACE SAUCE

$\frac{1}{2}$ pt Espagnole sauce	$\frac{1}{4}$ pt juices from roast meat *or* $\frac{1}{4}$ pt stock and 1 teasp good beef extract *or* meat glaze

Boil the sauce and meat juices together until well reduced. Skim off any fat before serving the sauce.
Serve with meat, poultry, game, etc.

ESPAGNOLE SAUCE

1 onion	2 oz flour
1 carrot	1 pt brown stock
2 oz mushrooms *or* mushroom trimmings	Bouquet garni 6 peppercorns 1 bay leaf
2 oz lean raw ham *or* bacon	$\frac{1}{4}$ pt tomato pulp Salt
2 oz butter *or* dripping	$\frac{1}{8}$ pt sherry (optional)

Slice the vegetables, chop the ham. Melt the fat and fry the ham for a few minutes and then, very slowly, the vegetables until they are golden-brown. Add the flour and continue frying very slowly till all is a rich brown. Add the stock, herbs and spices and stir till the sauce simmers; simmer for $\frac{1}{2}$ hr. Add the tomato pulp and simmer the sauce for a further $\frac{1}{2}$ hr. Wring the sauce through a tammy cloth or rub it through a fine hair or nylon sieve. Season, add the sherry, if used, and re-heat the sauce.

VELOUTÉ SAUCE

2 oz butter	1 pt good
6 button mush-rooms *or* mush-room trimmings	vegetable stock (*see above*) Salt and pepper
12 peppercorns	Lemon juice
A few parsley stalks	$\frac{1}{8}$–$\frac{1}{4}$ pt cream
2 oz flour	

Melt the butter in a saucepan and gently cook the mushrooms, peppercorns and parsley for 10 min. Add the flour and cook for a few minutes without browning it.

Stir in the stock, bring the sauce to simmering point and simmer for 1 hr. Wring the sauce through a tammy cloth or damp muslin. Season, add lemon juice, and reheat. Just at boiling point stir in the cream. The mushrooms may be rinsed and used as garnish for the dish.
For fish dishes, use fish stock.

SUPRÊME SAUCE

½ pt Velouté sauce	**Nutmeg to taste**
2 tablesp—⅛ pt cream	**Lemon juice**
1 egg yolk	**Salt and pepper**
½–1 oz butter	

Heat the Velouté sauce, preferably in a double boiler. Mix the egg yolk and cream, and stir into the sauce. Cook without boiling until the egg yolk thickens. Whisk in the butter, a small pat at a time. Add a pinch of nutmeg, a few drops of lemon juice, season and use the sauce at once.

TOMATO SAUCE

1 onion	**Salt and pepper**
1 small carrot	**Lemon juice**
1 oz bacon scraps *or* **bacon bone** *or* **rinds**	**Sugar**
½ oz butter *or* **margarine**	**Grated nutmeg**
4 medium-sized tomatoes, fresh, bottled *or* **canned**	
½ oz cornflour	
½ pt white stock *or* **liquid from canned** *or* **bottled tomatoes**	

Slice the onion and carrot. Put them into a saucepan with the bacon and fry them in the fat without browning them for 10 min. Slice and add the tomatoes and cook them for 5 min. Sprinkle in the cornflour, add the stock or juice, stir till the sauce boils. Simmer the sauce for 45 min. Rub the sauce through a hair or nylon sieve. Reheat, season and add lemon juice, sugar and nutmeg to taste.

ITALIAN SAUCE

½ pt Espagnole sauce	**⅛ pt white wine (optional)**
4 shallots	**Parsley stalks**
6 mushrooms	**Sprig of thyme**
1 tablesp olive oil	**1 bay leaf**
⅛ pt stock	**Salt and pepper**

Chop the shallots and mushrooms and cook them very gently for 10 min in the olive oil. Add the stock, wine (if used) herbs and spices and simmer gently until reduced by half. Add the Espagnole sauce and cook gently for 20 min. Season, and lift out the herbs.

PIQUANT SAUCE

½ pt brown sauce	**1 tablesp chopped gherkins**
1 onion *or* **2 shallots**	**1 dessertsp mushroom ketchup**
1 oz mushrooms	**½ teasp sugar (optional)**
1 bay leaf	
1 blade of mace	
2 tablesp vinegar	
1 tablesp halved capers	

Finely chop the onion or shallots, chop the mushrooms coarsely. Simmer the onion or shallots, the bay leaf and mace in the vinegar for 10 min. Add this mixture and the chopped mushrooms to the brown sauce and simmer till the mushrooms are soft. Add all the other ingredients. Do not strain the sauce but lift out bay leaf and mace. Serve with pork, mutton or vegetables.

MAYONNAISE, HAND-MADE

1–2 egg yolks	**Mixed vinegars to taste—if possible, 4 parts wine, vinegar** *or* **lemon juice, 2 parts tarragon and 1 part chilli vinegar**
Salt and pepper	
Mustard	
¼–½ pt best olive oil	

The eggs and oil should be at the same temperature and not too cold. In summer it is easier to make a good mayonnaise beginning with 2 egg yolks.

Remove every trace of egg white from the yolks. Put the yolks in a thick basin which will stand steady in spite of vigorous beating. Add to the egg yolks the pepper, salt and mustard to taste. Drop by drop, add the olive oil, beating or whisking vigorously all the time. As the mayonnaise thickens, the olive oil can be poured in a thin, steady stream but whisking must never slacken. When the mixture is really thick a few drops of vinegar or lemon juice stirred in will thin it again. Continue whisking in the oil, alternately with a little vinegar until the whole amount is added.

If the mayonnaise should curdle, break a fresh egg yolk into a clean basin and beat into this the curdled mixture just as the oil was added originally.

Various other ingredients are often added to mayonnaise, to give a different flavour and colour. They are useful when making a mixed hors-d'œuvre or any other dish of mixed products coated with mayonnaise, or they identify the different ingredients, and emphasise their variety.

Some variations are complex sauces in their own right. But it is hardly worth making these for light savoury dishes where, as a rule, only a small amount of each sauce is needed. So the following simple additions to plain Mayonnaise are suggested instead.

To ¼ pt mayonnaise, add:

) 2 tablesp concentrated tomato purée and sweet red pepper, chopped (Andalusian Sauce)
) 1 tablesp cooked spinach purée and 2 tablesp single cream (Green Mousseline Sauce)
) ½ teasp horseradish cream, 1 teasp each chopped parsley and chervil (Escoffier Sauce)
) 1 tablesp yogurt (or sour cream), ½ teasp chopped chives and a few drops each of Worcester Sauce and lemon juice (Gloucester Sauce)
) 1 oz mixed chopped fresh herbs, as many as you can get (Green Mayonnaise)

An electric blender makes almost foolproof mayonnaise. Use a whole egg instead of yolks and 2 tablesp vinegar. Put these into the goblet with the seasoning and whisk at high speed for 10 seconds. Still whisking, trickle in the oil gradually. The mixture

Savoury omelet with fish filling

will start to thicken after ¼ pt has gone in, and will not 'take' more than ½ pt.

White wine can be used instead of wine vinegar, and wine vinegar with a drop or two of Tabasco Sauce can replace the chilli vinegar.

FRENCH DRESSING

2–3 tablesp olive oil	1 tablesp wine vinegar
Pepper and salt	

Mix the oil and seasoning. Add the vinegar gradually, stirring constantly with a wooden spoon so that an emulsion is formed. Alternatively, make the sauce in a bottle with a tight stopper. Keep it in the fridge, and shake vigorously before use. French dressing will keep for several days if chilled. Lemon juice can be used in place of vinegar. Where suitable, orange or grapefruit juice can also be used.

A pinch of sugar, a little mustard and one or two drops of Worcester sauce can be added.

VINAIGRETTE SAUCE
This consists of a simple French dressing to which the following are added:

1 teasp finely chopped gherkin
½ teasp finely chopped shallot *or* **chives**
½ teasp finely chopped parsley
1 teasp finely chopped capers
½ teasp finely chopped tarragon and chervil (if available)

ASPIC JELLY

1 qt jellied veal stock	**2 egg whites and shells**
1 oz gelatine	**1 glass sherry**
Bouquet garni (parsley, thyme, bay leaf)	**(optional)**
	¼ pt vinegar
2 sticks of celery	

Let the stock become quite cold, and remove every particle of fat. Put it into a stewpan with the gelatine, herbs, celery cut into large pieces, the egg whites previously slightly beaten and the shells previously washed and dried. Whisk over heat until nearly boiling, then add the wine and vinegar. Then reduce the heat and simmer for about 10 min, strain till clear, and use.

MELBA SAUCE

To make Melba sauce pass the required quantity of fresh raspberries through a nylon sieve and sweeten with icing sugar. The sauce is not cooked.
Use as required.

MOCK MELBA SAUCE

½ oz arrowroot	**½ gill raspberry jam**
½ pt water	**Juice of ½ lemon**

Blend the arrowroot with a little of the water. Boil remaining water with the jam and lemon juice. Strain it on to the blended mixture, return to the pan and boil up, stirring all the time.
Cool before using.

BEURRE MANIÉ

The most economical way to thicken gravies, sauces and soups is with beurre manié or butter and flour kneaded together, usually in equal amounts. Work until smoothly blended, then drop small nuts of the mixture, one by one, into the near-boiling liquid. Whisk the sauce until it boils, by which time the thickening should be smoothly blended in.
Beurre manié will keep for several weeks in a refrigerator.

SAVOURY BUTTERS
General Method
Scald any herbs to be used, then chop all the ingredients. Crush and pound flavouring materials, or process in an electric blender. Cream butter, add the other items and mix until fully blended. Vary the amounts to suit your taste. Sieve the mixture if a smooth butter is required for piping, rosettes, curls, etc; or spread ¼–½ in thick on a plate and chill until firm, then cut out in round pats with a pastry cutter or shape into balls.
Use 2 oz butter, and salt and pepper to taste, with the ingredients below.

Anchovy Butter 6 bottled anchovies, lemon juice to taste (use no salt).

Curry Butter ½ teasp curry powder, teasp lemon juice.

Devilled Butter ¼ teasp each, cayenne pepper, white pepper, curry powder and ground ginger.

Garlic Butter 1–3 cloves blanched garlic, chopped parsley.

Herb Butter Good pinch each of dried thyme and parsley.

Lobster Butter 1 oz lobster coral and spawn (raw if to be used in a sauce or soup).

Maître D'Hôtel Butter 2 teasp finely chopped parsley, ½ teasp each chopped chervil and tarragon (optional), ½ teas lemon juice. Spread on a plate and chill after making, cut out round pats and use to top fish, steaks, etc.

Meunière or Noisette Butter Lemon juice. (Heat the butter until golden-fawn, add the lemon juice, and use hot.)

Mustard Butter 1–2 teasp French mustard.

Shrimp Butter ¼ pt cooked, shelled shrimp, pounded, lemon juice.

Tarragon Butter 1 teasp fresh tarragon, lemon juice.

Watercress Butter ¼ bunch finely chopped watercress.

GLAZES

To glaze is to make shiny. Pastry can be glazed with egg, sometimes called egg wash. Apricot or redcurrant glaze is used to brush over fruit tartlets, etc. Aspic jelly is used on hors-d'œuvres, cold fish dishes, etc, and meat glaze on both hot and cold meat dishes. Ham is sometimes glazed with syrup or jam. Icings such as Chocolate Glaze are used on cakes.

DEMI-GLAZE

Use clear stock suitable for consommé. Reduce it until slightly thick and 'tacky'.

GLAZE FOR MEAT DISHES, OR MEAT GLAZE

Strictly, you should reduce about 4 qt clear stock to about ¼ pt by continued boiling, uncovered. It is cheaper and quicker to add enough gelatine to strong stock to set it almost firm.

IMITATION MEAT GLAZE

Add 1¼ oz gelatine to ¼ pt cold water. Warm gently, stirring until dissolved. Without boiling, add 1 level teasp each of meat and yeast extract, and a little browning. Use hot to brush galantines, etc. Use soon; it does not keep well.

GLAZE FOR VEGETABLES

Make like Meat Glaze, using strong vegetable stock and yeast extract.

GLAZED VEGETABLES AS TRIMMINGS

Diced vegetables, slightly under-cooked The cooking liquid	Butter *or* margarine Granulated sugar

Drain the vegetables and put the cooking liquid into a saucepan. Melt the butter and sugar in it gently. Reduce if necessary, until there is just enough liquid to coat the vegetables. Add the vegetables, and toss. Simmer for a few minutes until they are well coated and beginning to colour.

GLAZES FOR PASTRY

(a) Egg wash or egg white glaze. Brush pastry with well-beaten egg or slightly beaten egg white before baking. For a deeper colour, use the yolk only, or the yolk and a little milk. Use for meat pies, patties, sausage rolls, etc.
(b) Sugar glazes. Fruit tarts, flans, puffs, etc, can be brushed lightly with cold water and dredged with castor sugar just before baking. Sugar syrup can also be used. For a thin coat of icing, brush with beaten egg white and dredge with castor sugar when nearly baked, or use thin glacé icing after baking. Buns and plain cakes can also be glazed with egg white and fine or coarsely crushed sugar.

BOUQUET GARNI or BUNCH OF FRESH HERBS or FAGGOT OF HERBS

1 sprig of thyme 1 sprig of marjoram 1 small sage leaf (optional) 1 strip of lemon rind (optional)	1 small bay leaf A few stalks of parsley A few chives (optional) Sprig of chervil (optional)

Tie all the herbs into a bunch with thick cotton or fine string. Alternatively the herbs may be tied in a small square of muslin. Add to soups, stews, sauces, etc, while they cook.

PARSLEY AS GARNISH

Parsley is perhaps the commonest trimming or garnish for all kinds of savoury dishes.

To blanch Bring a saucepan of water to the boil. Place the washed parsley sprigs in a strainer, dip it in the boiling water for a moment, then withdraw it and shake the parsley to dry it.

MAKING A FLAN CASE Read from left. 1, Lifting the pastry on a rolling pin. 2, Tucking pastry into flan case. 3, Filling the flan case with beans. 4, Lifting the flan case off the baked pastry shell.

To chop Blanch the parsley so that it keeps its greenness and Vitamin C. Wring it in a cloth to dry it. Cut off the stalks, and chop finely with a sharp knife, using a downward, not a 'sawing' stroke. Blanched parsley will not stain the chopping board.

To fry Immerse the washed and dried parsley in deep, hot fat for a few moments only.

CROÛTES AND CROÛTONS

A croûte is a fried or toasted slice of bread (round, square, etc) used as a base, usually for a savoury item such as a roast game bird or a meat mixture. Many hors-d'œuvres and snacks are served on small round croûtes or fingers of bread. Croûtes are also used as a garnish for a rich dish such as a salmi, their crispness contrasting with the sauce.

Croûtes should be cut from bread at least one day old, and should be $\frac{1}{4}-\frac{1}{2}$ in thick.

To fry croûtes

Use clarified butter or oil, and make sure that the first side is crisp and golden before turning.

To make toasted croûtes

Toast whole bread slices, and cut to shape after toasting, using a sharp knife.

TO MAKE CRESCENTS OR FLEURONS

Cut bread slices (or pastry) into circles with a pastry cutter. Then cut crescent moon shapes from these, with the same or a slightly smaller cutter.

Index

mond Paste   46
gels on Horseback   91
ple and Blue Cheese
vouries   99
ple and Raisin Lattice
rt   103
ple and Rice Stuffing   49
ple Loaf   79
ple Sauce   52
ricot Glaze   46
tichoke Bottoms, Stuffed
h Béchamel Sauce   18
tichokes, Globe with
ollandaise Sauce   11
pic Jelly   122
bergines with Poached
gs   101
ocado Pears with Prawns

con, Boiled with Olives

con Chops, Somerset Baked

con Olives   71
con Rolls, Grilled   79
nanas, Chartreuse of   40
nbury Cakes   114
th Buns   110
ttenburg Cakes   114
ans, French or Runner   36
chamel Sauce   119
ef à la Mode   30

Beef à la Nelson, Tournedos
of   31
Beef, Braised in Aspic   91
Beef Casserole, Sweet and
Sour   99
Beef Rossini, Tournedos of   13
Beef Strogonoff   30
Beurre Manié   122
Birthday Cake   67
Biscuits, Animal   66
Biscuits, Basic (Shrewsbury)
66
Biscuits, Eastertide   66
Biscuits, Mocha   114
Black Bun for Scot's New
Year's Eve   62
Bouquet Garni   123
Brandy Butter   53
Brandy or Rum Sauce   55
Brandy Snaps   80
Bread, Basic Milk   94
Bread, Cottage Loaves   97
Bread, Fried   79
Bread Knots   95
Bread Plait   95
Bread Rolls, Fancy   95
Bread Sauce   51
Bread Trefoils   95
Bread, Wholemeal   95
Broad Beans with Cream
Sauce   36
Broccoli   37

Brussels Sprouts, Boiled with
Chestnuts   53
Buns, Bath   110
Buns, Chelsea   110
Buns, Chocolate   111
Buns, Coconut   111
Buns, Ginger   111
Buns, Hot Cross   61
Buns, Lemon   111
Buns, London   111
Buns, Nut   111
Buns, Plain   110
Buns, Raspberry   111
Buns, Rock   111
Buns, Seed   111
Butter, Anchovy   122
Butter, Curry   122
Butter, Devilled   122
Butter, Garlic   122
Butter, Herb   122
Butter, Lobster   122
Butter, Maître D'Hôtel   122
Butter, Meunière or Noisette
122
Butter, Mustard   123
Butter, Shrimp   123
Butter, Tarragon   123
Butter, Watercress   123
Butters, Savoury   122

Cabbage, Red with Apples
37
Cake(s), Banbury   114

Cake(s) Basic Butter Sponge 68
Cake(s) Basic Large Cherry 112
Cake(s) Basic Large Fruit 112
Cake(s) Basic Large Ginger 112
Cake(s), Basic Large Lemon 112
Cake(s), Basic Large Madeira 112
Cake(s), Basic Large Rich 112
Cake(s) Basic Large Seed 112
Cake(s), Basic Large Sponge 114
Cake(s), Basic Small Cherry 66, 113
Cake(s) Basic Small Chocolate 66, 113
Cake(s), Basic Small Coconut 66, 113
Cake(s), Basic Small Lemon 66, 113
Cake(s), Basic Small Madeleines 66, 113
Cake(s), Basic Small Nut 66, 113
Cake(s), Basic Small Queen 66, 113
Cake(s), Basic Small Rich 65, 112
Cake(s), Basic Small Sponge 64
Cake(s), Battenburg 115
Cake(s), Birthday 67
Cake(s), Butterfly Orange 66
Cake(s), Christening 58
Cake(s), Christmas 56
Cake(s), Christmas Yule Log 59
Cake(s), Coffee Walnut 116
Cake(s), Crown Celebration 58
Cake(s), Drum Children's Party 58
Cake(s), Dundee 114
Cake(s), Easter Egg 60
Cake(s), Fairy Cottage Children's Party 59
Cake(s), Festive Gâteau 62
Cake(s), Genoese 57

Cake(s), Hallowe'en Party 59
Cake(s), Icebox 62
Cake(s), Lardy 109
Cake(s), Lemon or Orange Sandwich 114
Cake(s), Maypole Children's Party 58
Cake(s), Mother's 60
Cake(s), Pavlova 21
Cake(s), Simnel 60
Cake(s), Small Iced or French 115
Cake(s), Small Plain 64
Cake(s), Twelfth Night 61
Cake(s), Valentine's 61
Cake(s), Victoria Sandwich 113
Cake(s), Wedding 45
Caramel Custard 39
Carrot Salad 83
Carrots, Glazed 54
Cauliflower Salad, Cooked 84
Cauliflower with White Sauce 54
Celery, Braised 38
Cheese and Onion Pie 76
Cheese, Blue and Apple Savouries 99
Cheese Flan 78
Chestnuts au Jus 53
Chicken, Cold, Garnished 91
Chicken Duchesse, Curried 35
Chicken Livers, Devilled 107
Chicken, Roast, French Style 34
Chicken Tartlets 99
Chicken Vol-au-Vent 75
Chicken with Suprême Sauce 34
Chocolate Choux or Profiteroles 38
Chocolate Sauce 39
Chou Pastry 39
Christening Cake 58
Christmas Cake 56
Christmas Pudding 54
Coconut Pyramids 67
Consommé Madrilène 12
Consommé Rosé 88
Coq au Vin 34
Crab, Dressed 24

Cranberry Sauce 51
Cream Cheese Flan 91
Crème Brulée 42
Crêpes Suzette 22
Crescents 124
Croûtes and Croûtons 124
Crunchies 115
Cucumber and Seafood Roll 88
Cucumber Cream Soup 24
Cucumber, Steamed with White Sauce 18
Curry Sauce, Mild 35
Custard, Basic with Eggs 4
Custard, Caramel 39
Custard, Confectioners' 94
Custard, Rich 43
Custards for Ice Cream 43

Dates 22
Devils on Horseback 71
Duckling, Stuffed 35
Dundee Cake 114

Easter Egg Cake 60
Eggs, Scotch 78
Espagnole Sauce 119

Festive Gâteau 62
Fleurons 124
French Dressing 121
Fried Bread 79
Frosting, American 68
Fruit Cake, Basic Large 11
Fruit Flan 41
Fruit Punch 80
Fruit Salad 55
Fudge 68

Gammon, Boiled with Olives 33
Gammon Steaks with Rice
Garnish 34, 91, 107
Garnishes, Savoury Scandinavian 87
Genoese Cake 57
Ginger Cake, Basic Large 112
Ginger Snaps 67
Ginger Twists 97
Gingerbread, Rich Dark 6
Glaze(s) 115, 123
Glaze, Apricot 46
Glaze for Pastry 123

laze for Vegetables 123
laze, Imitation Meat 123
oose, Roast 52
rapefruit Baskets 23
rapefruit, Tuna Salad in 48
ravy 51
rill, Mixed 80
rouse Pie 17

alibut, Cooked, Coquilles f 26
alibut with Orange and
/atercress Salad 91
am Mousse 89
am Rolls 74
amburgers 74
awaiian Dreams 20
errings, Rollmop 88
erbs, Bunch of Fresh 123
erbs, Faggots of 123
ollandaise Sauce 12
ot Cross Buns 61

e Cream, Chocolate 43
:e Cream, Coffee 43
:e Cream, Raspberry 43
:e Cream, Strawberry 43
:e Cream, Vanilla 43
:e, Lemon Water 86
:es, Moulding 43
:es, Syrup for Water 86
:ing, Almond 68
:ing Butter 68, 70
:ing, Chocolate 68
:ing, Coffee 68
:ing, Lemon 68
:ing, Orange 68
:ing, Royal 68
:ing, Vanilla 68
:ing, Walnut 68
alian Sauce 120

lly, Aspic 122
lly, Lemon 41

edgeree 71
idneys, Grilled 107
idneys with Italian Sauce
irsch Sauce 42
nickerbocker Glory 93

amb, Crown Roast of, ith Saffron Rice 14

Lamb Cutlets en Papillotes 31
Lamb Kebabs 31
Lamb or Mutton Pies,
Cumberland 94
Lemon Jelly 41
Lemon Meringue Pie 107
Lemon or Orange Sorbet 86
Liver 'Bites', Grilled 78
Liver Pâté 89
Lobster, Devilled 13
Lobster, Dressed 30
Lobster, How to Boil 15
Lobster, How to Choose 15
Lobster, How to Prepare 15
Lobster Mayonnaise 30
Lobster Thermidor 13

Macaroni au Gratin with Bacon Rolls 78
Madeira Cake, Basic Large
112
Marshmallows 70
Marzipan 22
Mayonnaise, Hand-Made
120
Meat Balls 76
Melon 48
Melting Moments 67
Mince Pies 55
Mincemeat 56
Minestrone 100
Moules Marinières 27
Mousse, Ham 89
Mousses, Cold 89
Mullet, Grey en Papillotes 15
Mulligatawny Soup 98
Mushrooms, Grilled 83
Mussels, Florentine 27
Mussels, To Choose 27
Mussels, To Prepare 27
Mutton or Lamb Pies,
Cumberland 94

Nougat 70

Omelette, Cheese 106
Omelette, English 107
Omelette, Fines Herbes 106
Omelette, French 106
Omelette, Kidney 106
Omelette, Mushroom 106
Omelette, Onion 106
Omelette, Shellfish 106
Omelette, Spanish 107

Omelettes, Savoury 106
Onion Rings 79
Onions, Stuffed Braised 50
Orange Salad 83

Pancake Batter 82
Pancakes, Savoury with
Bacon 82
Pancakes, Savoury with
Cheese 82
Pancakes, Savoury with Tuna
and Prawns 82
Pancakes, Stuffed with
Kidneys in Port Wine 82
Pancakes, Sweet 85
Parsley as Garnish 123
Pastry, Chou 39
Pastry, Crumb 117
Pastry, Puff 118
Pastry, Short and Rich Short
Crust 117
Pâté Sucrée 117
Patties 89
Patties, Chicken 90
Patties, Mushroom 90
Patties, Sardine 90
Patties, Sausage and Apple
90
Pavlova Cake 21
Peaches Preserved in Brandy
22
Pears Filled with Nut and
Date Salad 102
Peas, Green 54
Peas, Green, French Style 18
Pease Pudding 98
Peppermint Creams 22
Petits Fours 56, 57
Pheasant, Salmi of 16
Pie, Cheese and Onion 76
Pie, Grouse 17
Pie, Lemon Meringue 107
Pie, Mince 55
Piquant Sauce 120
Pork Casserole, Boston 106
Pork Chops, Braised in Cider
32
Potato Chips 19
Potato Crisps 63
Potato Salad 84
Potato Straws 19
Potatoes, Anna 18
Potatoes, Baked and Stuffed
74

Potatoes, Baked in their Jackets 98
Potatoes, Boiled 38
Potatoes, Creamed 38
Potatoes, Mashed 38
Potatoes, Sautéed 19
Prawn Cocktail, 23
Prawns, Dublin Bay
Provençale 100
Profiteroles 38
Pudding, Christmas 54

Red Cabbage with Apples 37
Rice and Apple Stuffing 49
Rice Salad 83
Risotto 102
Rum Sauce 55

Sage and Onion Stuffing 52
Salad, Carrot 83
Salad, Cooked Cauliflower 84
Salad, Fruit 55
Salad, Mixed Summer Vegetable 92
Salad, Mixed Winter Vegetable 93
Salad, Orange 83
Salad, Potato 84
Salad, Rice 83
Salad, Tomato 84
Salad, Tuna in Grapefruit 48
Salmon Cutlets, Mornay 30
Sandwich Fillings 87
Sandwiches 86
Sandwiches, Open 87
Sauce, Apple 52
Sauce, Basic Brown 118
Sauce, Basic White 118
Sauce, Béchamel 119
Sauce, Brandy 55
Sauce, Bread 51
Sauce, Chocolate 39
Sauce, Cranberry 51
Sauce, Demi-Glace 119
Sauce, Espagnole 119
Sauce, Hollandaise 12
Sauce, Italian 120
Sauce, Kirsch 42
Sauce, Melba 122
Sauce, Mild Curry 35

Sauce, Mock Melba 122
Sauce, Piquant 120
Sauce, Rum 55
Sauce, Suprême 120
Sauce, Tartare 106
Sauce, Tomato 120
Sauce, Velouté 119
Sauce, Vinaigrette 122
Sausage and Apple Mash 75
Sausage Rolls 63
Sausage Snacks 63
Sausage Stuffing 51
Sausages, Cocktail 75
Sausages, Frankfurters 75
Sausages, Large 75
Savarin 42
Scallops en Brochette 14
Scampi, Fried with Tartare Sauce 103
Scampi or Dublin Bay Prawns Provençale 100
Scandinavian Tea Ring 111
Scones, Basic Plain 108
Scones, Cheese 108
Scones, Fruit 108
Scones, Griddle 108
Scones, Nut 109
Scones, Sweet 109
Scones, Treacle 109
Scones, Wholemeal 109
Scotch Eggs 78
Seafood and Cucumber Rolls 88
Sea-Food Chowder 26
Sea-Food Flan 74
Shortbread, Scottish 111
Shortcake, Strawberry 39
Shrimps, Potted 24
Simnel Cake 60
Sole à la Portugaise 28
Sole, Fillets of, with Cream Sauce 28
Sorbet, Lemon or Orange 86
Soufflé, Milanese 19
Soup, Bortsch, Polish or Russian Beetroot 26
Soup, Cucumber Cream 24
Soup, French Onion 103
Soup, Minestrone 100
Soup, Mulligatawny 98
Soup, Tomato 48
Spinach, Poached 18
Sponge Cake, Basic Butter 68

Sponge Cake, Basic Large 114
Steak, Châteaubriand 13
Stuffing 35
Stuffing, Apple and Rice 4?
Stuffing, Sage and Onion 5?
Stuffing, Sausage 51
Suprême Sauce 120

Tartare Sauce 106
Tomato Salad 84
Tomato Sauce 120
Tomato Soup 48
Tomatoes, Baked 83
Trifle 79
Trout 'Au Bleu' 15
Trout en Papillotes 15
Trout Meunière 27
Tuna Salad in Grapefruit 4?
Turbot, Coquilles of Cooked 26
Turkey or Chicken Tartlets 99
Turkey, Roast with Apple an? Rice Stuffing 49
Turkey, Roast with Chestnut? 51

Vanilla Slices 115
Vegetable Salad, Mixed Summer 92
Vegetable Salad, Mixed Winter 93
Vegetables, Cooked Mixed 36
Vegetables, Glazed as Trimmings 123
Velouté Sauce 119
Victoria Sandwich 113
Vinaigrette Sauce 122
Vol-au-Vents 89
Vol-au-Vents, Chicken 90
Vol-au-Vents, Mushroom 9?
Vol-au-Vents, Sardine 90
Vol-au-Vents, Sausage and Apple 90

Waffles 102
Water Ice, Lemon 86
Water Ices, Syrup for 86
Wedding Cake 45
Welsh Rarebit 107
Whitebait, Fried 26
Wiener Schnitzel 31